RAMANUJAR

The Life and Ideas of Ramanuja

INDIRA PARTHASARATHY

Translated from Tamil by
T. SRIRAMAN

Critical Introduction and Commentary by
C.T. INDRA

OXFORD
UNIVERSITY PRESS

OXFORD
UNIVERSITY PRESS

YMCA Library Building, Jai Singh Road, New Delhi 110 001

Oxford University Press is a department of the University of Oxford. It furthers
the University's objective of excellence in research, scholarship, and education
by publishing worldwide in

Oxford   New York

Auckland   Cape Town   Dar es Salaam   Hong Kong   Karachi
Kuala Lumpur   Madrid   Melbourne   Mexico City   Nairobi
New Delhi   Shanghai   Taipei   Toronto

With offices in

Argentina   Austria   Brazil   Chile   Czech Republic   France   Greece
Guatemala   Hungary   Italy   Japan   Poland   Portugal   Singapore
South Korea   Switzerland   Thailand   Turkey   Ukraine   Vietnam

Oxford is a registered trade mark of Oxford University Press
in the UK and in certain other countries

Published in India by Oxford University Press, New Delhi

ISBN-13: 978-0-19-569161-0
ISBN-10: 0-19-569161-X

Typeset in AmericanGaramond
by Mindways Design, Delhi 110 035
Printed in India by De Unique, New Delhi 110 018
Published by Oxford University Press
YMCA Library Building, Jai Singh Road, New Delhi 110 001

C.T. Indra and T. Sriraman
dedicate this book to their Acharyan,
the late Professor V.S. Seturaman

CONTENTS

ACKNOWLEDGEMENTS

I am deeply grateful to Mr Hariharan and Dr Meenakshi Hariharan for taking a keen interest in this work and fetching invaluable materials on Ramanuja from various libraries. Meenakshi also acted as my sounding board as well as amanuensis during the year-long struggle to write a critique and textual commentary on the play. I am grateful to Professor A.A. Manavalan for obtaining a copy of Professor M.S. Govindasamy's Endowment lecture and to my teacher Professor S.N. Kandasamy for providing me with a published version of the same lecture just in time. My thanks are due to Professor V.K.N.S. Raghavan of the Vaishnavism department at the University of Madras for explaining certain recondite passages of Vaishnavism. Professor M. Narasimhachary, the first professor of Vaishnavism at the University of Madras, graciously gifted me a copy of his biography of Ramanuja. My sincere thanks to a devout Sri Vaishnavite who would like to remain unnamed, for the precious professional help of furnishing me with a copy of the *Guruparamparai Prabhavam 6000*. Last but not the least, I am indebted to Dr Chitra Madhavan who directed me to the important epigraphical work by B.R. Gopal, *Sri Ramanuja in Karnataka*, which helped give a fresh direction to my critique.

C.T. Indra

I would like to thank Sri Indira Parthasarathy for kindly permitting me to translate this play. I am grateful to Smt Sowbhaghyalakshmi, principal of Sri Sadagopan Tirunarayanaswami Divya Prabandha Pathasala, Chennai, for according permission to use the translations of *pasurams* from the late Srirama Bharati's *The Sacred Book of Four Thousand*. I thank my brother-in-law, Sri V.S. Viraraghavan, for his help in resolving several difficulties that I encountered in the course of translation and for the constant affectionate encouragement that he has given me.

T. Sriraman

LIST OF ABBREVIATIONS

AKVG	:	Alkondavilli Govindacharya
GPP 6000	:	*Guruparamparai Prabhavam 6000* by Pinpalagiya Perumal Jiyar
JTS	:	*Journal of Tamil Studies*, vol. 67, June 2005.
MSG	:	M.S. Govindasamy
NDP	:	*Nalayira Divya Prabandham*

HAGIOGRAPHY REVISITED

The subject of hagiography is critically interesting, especially in the context of the radically changing social scenario in our country in the post-modern period. Indeed, education has felt the greatest impact of such shifts in values and privileges. Recent literatures and literary studies echo these paradigm shifts. Literatures in our own languages, and also in English, frontally deal with pressing issues that rack the elite and the common man alike. Older forms of writing have been reread to interrogate their original contexts of production and reception. Hagiography has become a tool for serious writers to re-examine received ideas on wisdom, sanctity, and liberation.

The Concise Longman Dictonary, which traces the word 'hagiography' to the Greek root *hagios* meaning (1) holy and (2) saints, defines the term as (a) biography of saints or venerated people and (b) idealizing or idolizing biography. The *Oxford Advanced Learner's Dictionary* also gives similar definitions. However, there seems to be a more critical view of the mode in its second definition which says: 'biographical writing that is too full of praise for its subject'. Such recent dictionary definitions reflect a suspicion of any mega claim about any person that militates against our sense of credibility.

The concept of hagiography is rooted in our sense of wonder at human beings who have shown extraordinary vision and marvellous power in transcending their mortal limitations. The work that results from this sense of wonder is not an intellectual exercise or strain. The experience pertains to the emotions and sensibilities of the human personality. It cannot be contained by the power of reason. We need not assume that such an experience is true of only the popular/unlettered mind. The appeal of the suprarational is as much to the avowedly educated and cultivated.

The conception of the suprarational human person has led to the type of narrative which has come to be designated as 'hagiography'. The genre has developed its own grammar and methodology. It is predicated on a mode of storytelling which may be linear but its significance cannot be grasped at the temporal level. It takes recourse to non-rational modes of representation of events and actions. One should say it finds the rational mode of apprehension inadequate for grasping the full import of the actions of a personality who is larger than life. It has a natural proclivity towards miracles. Often action is governed by a *deus ex machina* or divine intervention, which resolves insurmountable problems. Hence, the structure of such narratives is embedded in a specific cultural milieu in which a transvaluation renders the temporal, existential situation non-essential. Hagiography can also be used to refer to the modern discipline of studying such writings.

Thus hagiographies operate in dual spheres: the religious and the social. Because of its embeddedness in the religio-cultural matrix, the genre has had its provenance both in the East and in the West and can boast of an impressive genealogy across cultures—Hindu, Buddhist, Jain, Christian, and Islamic.

The aim of the Christian hagiographers was not to produce biography in the modern sense, but rather to portray a saint as an exemplar of the Christian life. Hagiography has the power to create solidarity within a community, a people, and empower them in interesting ways. The narrative is aimed at giving a sense of belief and a value system to a people. It results in cohesive thinking and one of the objectives seems to be to create a sense of acceptance of the world-view or metaphysic or principle of order so propounded. Therefore, it aims to achieve that willing suspension of disbelief which constitutes faith in the minds of the members of the group or community.

The post-modern and post-colonial world has taken a keen interest in the tradition and mode of hagiography. Intellectuals have studied the processes of legitimizing power in various societies, which include appealing to religious sentiments and susceptibilities. That certainly is the province of hagiography. In the literary field, writers have redeployed the form of hagiography to study the process of securing and consolidating power and, in general, the hegemonic principle and its operations. A hagiographic text, or the genre of hagiography itself, can become an intertext to study the responses generated by the mode in previous eras and sometimes to produce a counter-response. What is produced through this intertextual mode may take two directions: (1) demythologizing, that is stripping the stuff of its supernatural frills and humanizing the whole—the personality, the action, its significance. This demythologizing need not be a dehumanizing exercise. It may aim at affirming the humanist values embodied even while discarding the legitimizing apparatus; (2) desacralizing, that is denouncing, rejecting the very positing of sanctity as a value which is at the heart of hagiography. This second mode often results in turning the genre into satire. It partakes of the deconstructive spirit of much contemporary thinking. There is nothing to affirm except perhaps the presence of a void.

Thus religion and belief are the loci which are interrogated through revisiting hagiography. In these loci we find the function of the hagiographer overlapping with that of the historian/chronicler and the artist. Hence we find the emergence of new kinds of chroniclers and artists forging their critiques in the smithy of hagiography.

J.B. Carman, Professor of Comparative Religion at Harvard University, has examined the approach of the phenomenologist vis-à-vis the hagiographer. The former studies a chosen religion as an outsider. He can never experience a religion not his own as a power in life. If he could really do so, he would become an adherent of that religion and his study as a phenomenologist would come to an end. Carman attempts to relate the phenomenological and historical approaches to the study of religion. He refers, in this context, to the Dutch model of the phenomenology of religion, summed up by the renowned scholar W. Brede Kristensen. Kristensen set forth two requirements for the phenomenological approach to religion: self-denial, negatively speaking, letting the believer himself speak without mixing our praise or blame with what he says; positively, having an attitude of sympathetic understanding towards the alien faith (Carman 1974: 3). Thus his two rules are the attitudes of *epoché*, that is restraint, and *einfuhlen*, that is sympathy (ibid.: 5). The latter pulls you towards the subject, the former holds you in check! Carman notes that questions of truth and value are put aside in the phenomenology of religion, whereas in the theological approach they are the prime denominators, as pointed out by Hendrik Kraemer. Carman draws an analogy between grammar and phenomenology arguing that 'there is a pattern to be discovered and that its discovery is possible not by taking some average of the believers of that religion or speaker of that language but by concentrating on those in whom that pattern really lives' (ibid.:10). According to van der Leeuw, history is to be distinguished from phenomenology because there is a limit to the number of religions that an observer can know well enough (cited in ibid.:5). Using these philosophical and hermeneutical models in contemporary times, Carman proposes that we constitute a post-colonial perspective. He points out that because of the impact of phenomenology, an intercultural and interreligious understanding has emerged and this is relatively new in human history.

What Carman recommends is partly useful for our purpose in understanding how and why hagiography has been redeployed by some of the writers in India in the recent past. The counternarratives that emerge from them call for eschewing both restraint and sympathy!

The personality of Ramanuja, the renowned spiritual teacher who represented the school of qualified monism in Hindu philosophy known in professional philosophical discourse as *Visishtadvaita*, has inspired many to tell again and again the story of his life, which is one of profound aspiration and youthful enthusiasm to embrace the whole of humanity irrespective of caste, creed, and status, and take them to the feet of the supreme Lord to receive His grace and attain ineffable delight. His story has been told in the form of verse, in cryptic narration, in the Manipravala mode, which is a mixture of Sanskrit and Tamil; it has been retold in the form of a play and very recently in the form of verse biography (Vaali's *Ramanuja Kavyam*, 2003). It has been told in Sanskrit, in Tamil, in Telugu, in Bengali, and in English (for example Alkondavilli Govindacharya's *Sri Ramanujacharya*, 1906). It has been part of compendiums on the tradition of Vaishnava Acharyas (for example *Acharya Vaibhavam*, 1992). The 1899 Bengali biography by Sri Ramakrishnananda was translated into English (1949–54). There have been English biographies in modern times by scholars of Vaishnavism (for example M. Narasimhachary's *Sri Ramanuja* published by the Sahitya Akademi in 2004).

Most of these retellings show remarkable agreement in depicting the crucial events of his life, his personality traits, and his progressive actions which had far-reaching consequences for orthodox Hindu religious and social organization in the centuries that followed. Many western scholars, especially those with a Christian theological background, have evinced interest in Ramanuja's thought and written perceptively about his life and contribution (for example Carman's *The Theology of Ramanuja*, 1974). Indian Christian scholars have also taken a deep interest in Ramanuja's life and theology (for example Cyril Veliath's *The Mysticism of Ramanuja*, 1993). The latest biography, by the poet Vaali (*Ramanuja Kavyam*, 2003), does not merely retell the story of Ramanuja but sees him in the context of modern social reformers and thinkers like Periyar in Tamil Nadu and Ambedkar in Maharashtra. Let us look at the life and times of this illustrious man.

Life of Ramanuja in Legend and History

The Rich Tapestry of Legends

Ramanuja was born in Sriperumpudur near Madras city, now called Chennai, in northern Tamil Nadu in the eleventh century. According to legend he was born in 1017 and lived for 120 years, that is he died in 1137. He was born in an orthodox Vadama Brahmin family given to Vedic studies. His father was Asuri Somayaji Kesava Dikshitar and his name suggests the Vedic background of his clan. His mother was Kantimati. When he grew up, Ramanuja first went to the great teacher of Vedanta in Thirupputkuzhi near Kanchipuram, Yadava Prakasa. He learnt the scriptures while in devout personal service of his guru. On one occasion, when Yadava interpreted the well-known passage from *Taittiriya Upanishad*, '*Satyam Gnanam Anantam Brahma*', Ramanuja ventured to suggest that the passage meant 'not that Brahman is satyam, gnanam and anantam [truth, wisdom, infinitude] but that Brahman has them as Its qualities and that they are attributes which co-exist in Brahman without mutual contradiction, just as redness, softness and perfume could harmoniously co-exist in a flower' (Yamunacharya 1988: 4). It is said that the teacher was much annoyed by the impertinence of the young student. On another occasion, the teacher was commenting on a passage from *Chandogya Upanishad*, citing Sankara's linguistic explanation of the verse: Brahman had his eyes red as the posterior of the monkey. Ramanuja was much pained by the unseemly comparison and shed tears silently. Yadava became aware of Ramanuja's emotional disturbance. He asked for an explanation and Ramanuja politely gave the reason and went on to offer a more proper reading of the verse *'Tasya Yatha Kapyasam Pundarikameva makshini'*: *"Ka"* means water and *"pibati"* signifies drinking, *"kapi"* means that which drinks water, the sun or the lotus stalk. *"Asa"* is to open, *"Pundarika"* is the lotus. And therefore, the import of the passage is that God has eyes like the lotus which blooms before the morning sun' (ibid.: 5). Yadava Prakasa was naturally offended at being contradicted. According to legend, after this incident he came to fear Ramanuja's intelligence, which he thought might harm the interest of the school of Advaita and hence decided to eliminate him when he took him on a holy tour up north. With the timely help of his cousin Govinda, who was also studying with him, Ramanuja survived the plot and eventually returned to Kanchipuram through divine intervention in the form of a fowler couple in the forest.

Ramanuja went to Kanchi Purna (known in Tamil as Tirukkacchi Nambi) who was a disciple of the renowned Vaishnava Acharya Yamunacharya known in Tamil as Alavandar, and whose job was to fan the deity Lord Varadaraja in the temple at Kanchipuram. Kanchi Purna asked Ramanuja to keep serving the Lord by bringing water from a well at some distance. (Even today, the well from which Ramanuja drew water for use in the temple exists and is called 'Salaikinaru', that is the well on the roadside.) Ramanuja was married to Thanjamamba (in Sanskrit, 'Rakshakamba') who hailed from an affluent orthodox family. However, she could not share the spiritual aspirations and zeal of her husband, particularly his respect for Kanchi Purna because the latter was, in spite of his spiritual attainments, a Vaisya, lower in the varna or caste system. On one occasion, when Ramanuja invited Kanchi Purna for lunch, being conscious of her high caste ancestry, she fed Kanchi Purna in the front portion of the house and used a stick to remove the plantain leaf on which the food was served, and then ritualistically cleaned the place sprinkling cow dung and water. When Ramanuja came to know of this, he was deeply offended by her *Bhagavata apacharam* (insult to a devotee of the Lord) which is against the spirit of a Vaishnava. On another occasion, he was having his customary oil massage by a poor, non-Brahmin. Noticing his fatigue, Ramanuja wanted to know if the masseur was ill. He learnt that the man was starving. At once, Ramanuja directed his wife to give him some food, even if it was leftovers. She replied that there was none. Ramanuja, doubting her, went into the kitchen to find that there was indeed some food left. He was quite angered by her lack of compassion which was a sin.

He continued to learn from Kanchi Purna whatever the latter could impart within the limitations imposed by his caste. One day, he asked Kanchi Purna to find out from Lord Varadaraja at the temple the path he should pursue. Legend has it that the Lord gave six instructions, one of which was that Ramanuja should go to Srirangam and learn from Maha Purna (in Tamil, Periya Nambi), one of the prime disciples of Alavandar. When Ramanuja was proceeding towards Srirangam, Maha Purna himself was coming to Kanchi to meet him on instructions from his Guru. They met at Madurantakam. Maha Purna initiated Ramanuja into the Sri Vaishnava mode of life by administering the *panchasamskara* to him (including branding on his upper arms/shoulders the sacred images of the conch and discus held by Lord Maha Vishnu in Hindu iconography) and teaching him the mantras. Ramanuja brought Maha Purna and his wife back with him to Kanchi and entertained them as guests. For six months, Maha Purna stayed with Ramanuja and taught him *Divya Prabandham* and other Vaishnava texts. Ramanuja's wife, however, did not take kindly to the elderly couple. A silly quarrel arose on one occasion when both the women were drawing water from the well. Maha Purna's wife's pot touched Ramanuja's wife's which was construed by the former as offensive to her ritual purity. She spoke rudely to Maha Purna's wife, taunting her about her lower social and economic status. When Maha Purna came to hear of this, he chided his wife for giving cause for such an outburst and decided to go back to Srirangam without informing Ramanuja. When Ramanuja came to know of what had happened, he was furious with his wife for her conduct, her superciliousness, her arrogance born of caste, class, and education. He decided that he could not continue the life of a *grhasta* (householder) and also pursue his spiritual aspirations. One version says that he sent his wife to her parents' home to attend her brother's wedding, promising to follow her, and then left his house forever to become a renunciate. Another version says, he told her to her face that she was not fit to be his wife and walked out of the house. Variations apart, Ramanuja went to Lord Varadaraja temple, prayed to the deity, and took *sanyasa* straight from Him, that is he was not

initiated by any guru but became a self-made acharya—
swayamacharya. The Lord gave him the name 'Ramanuja Muni'.

Very soon, because of his transparent spirituality and eagerness to
lead humanity on an enlightened path of salvation, he started attracting
young and eager disciples. A very rich man from the village of Kuram
near Kanchipuram, Kuresa, renounced all his wealth and joined
Ramanuja's ashram with his erudite wife Andal Amma. Ramanuja's
sister's son Dasarathi also joined him and the two men came to be
immortalized in legends, hagiographies, and even epigraphs as
Kurattazhwan and Mudaliyandan—Azhwan and Andan for short.
Although Ramanuja was in his own right a pontiff, his infinite humility
and eagerness prompted him to learn the full import of the Sri
Vaishnava doctrine first propounded by Sage Nathamuni in the tenth
century at Kattumannar Koil, near Chidambaram town, and later
disseminated by his grandson Alavandar. Alavandar had once seen from
a distance the young Ramanuja in the company of his guru Yadava
Prakasa, on a visit to Kanchi. Now ageing and ailing, Alavandar yearned
to leave the legacy of his Vaishnavite creed as well as the charge of the
pontificate at Srirangam to Ramanuja. Hence, he sent Maha Purna to
fetch Ramanuja. By the time both Maha Purna and Ramanuja hastened
to Srirangam, Alavandar had died and preparations were going on for
his interment at Tirukkarambanthurai on the banks of the Kaveri.
Deeply disturbed by the turn of events though he was, Ramanuja
noticed a curious sight: three of Alavandar's fingers were closed. When
Ramanuja wanted to know its import, the disciples standing around
replied that they did not know of any specific wishes of their guru
except that he used to say: (a) that sage Veda Vyasa who wrote the
Mahabharata and his father sage Parasara who wrote the *Vishnupurana*
should be remembered and commemorated for posterity; (b) that the
greatness of Nammazhwar, the mystic hymnist from Azhwar
Thirunagari down south, must be proclaimed; (c) a commentary
(*bhashya*) on Vyasa's recondite work *Brahmasutra* must be written along
the lines of Sri Vaishnava thought. Ramanuja heard this and declared to
all assembled that he would endeavour to fulfil all the three wishes of
the departed acharya. The three fingers immediately straightened.
Everyone was convinced that Ramanuja was to be the successor of
Alavandar. But Ramanuja, sorely disappointed that he could not see
the great man alive, returned to Kanchipuram in frustration.

At Kanchipuram, he continued to spread the Sri Vaishnava faith, and held keen discourse with his disciples. Thus fully groomed Ramanuja was rising in stature, surrounded by eminent disciples like Kuresa, Dasarathi, and Nadathur Azhvan (another nephew). Even his old teacher, Yadava Prakasa, impelled by his mother, became a disciple. Ramanuja gave him the name Govinda Jiyar and he subsequently wrote a book of rules for ascetics, *Yatidharma Samuccya*. The disciples of Yamuna at Srirangam sorely needed leadership and Lord Ranganatha sent a message to Lord Varada to relieve Ramanuja of his duties at Kanchi so that he could head the pontificate at Srirangam. Captivated by the divine singing of the emissary Tiruvarangap Perumal Arayar, the cantor, the Lord at Kanchi granted the boon sought which was none other than Ramanuja himself. Thus Ramanuja assumed charge of the Srirangam *mutt*.

It is a remarkable fact of his life and career that Ramanuja, who was never a direct student of Alavandar, learnt from five of his well-known disciples important doctrinal, mystical, and literary texts. Maha Purna taught him the Tamil hymns called Dravida Vedas or *Nalayira Divya Prabandham* and certain Vaishnava tenets. Ramanuja was directed by Kanchi Purna to go to Thirukottiyur, south of Madurai, to seek Ghoshti Purna (in Tamil, Thirukkottiyur Nambi), a Vedic scholar and another disciple of Alavandar, to learn the inner import of three very sacred Vaishnava texts (i) *Ashtakshari* or the eight-syllabled adoration of Vishnu, *Om Namo Narayanaya*, (ii) the *Dvaya mantra*, and (iii) the *charama sloka* from the Bhagavadgita.[1] Ramanuja went seventeen times to the southern town and was every time sent back. He was asked to come by himself the eighteenth time taking with him only his pennant and staff, to learn the secret import of these three texts. Ramanuja chose to go with his inseparable companions Kuresa and Mudaliyandan. When arraigned by Ghoshti Purna for this blatant violation, Ramanuja famously replied that he had indeed come with his pennant and staff as a sanyasi ('I have come with my *pavitram* and *tridandam*'). Ghoshti Purna however took him separately and taught him the embedded import of Ashtaksharimantra forbidding him from sharing it with anyone, warning him that if he did so, he would go to hell. Ramanuja was so enthused by the idea that this mantra could bring salvation that he thought that instead of keeping it to himself, he should share it with fellow human beings and help them cross the ocean of existence. Resolved, he climbed the inner tower of the Saumya Narayana temple at Thirukkottiyur, reached the second tier, called out to all those around, uttered the mantra and its import, and exhorted them to follow it. He did not mind himself being damned in the process. When Ghoshti Purna came to know of this sacrilege, he called Ramanuja to explain and reminded him of the consequences of his transgression. Ramanuja replied cheerfully that he was prompted by the prospect of so many people being redeemed and in any case he knew he would not be thrown out of grace because he had already clutched the feet of Ghoshti Purna! His witty but sincere reply so overwhelmed Ghoshti Purna that he acknowledged with open heart that he did not have the compassion of the young Ramanuja. He went on to declare that henceforth what was *paramavaidika siddhantha* (ultra-orthodox doctrine) would be called Emberumanar *darsanam* or the philosophy of Emberumanar, a title he bestowed on Ramanuja which means 'our leader'.

Ramanuja returned in triumph to Srirangam and continued his mission. He visited the hill sanctum at Tirupati which was at the northern limit of the Tamil/Dravida country. He learnt the Ramayana from his maternal uncle and another pupil of Alavandar, Sri Saila Purna (in Tamil, Periya Tirumalai Nambi). He learnt Nammalvar's *Tiruvaimozhi* from yet another disciple of Alavandar, Maladhara (in Tamil, Tirumalai Andan). When, on one occasion, he offered a different interpretation of a Tamil verse from what Maladhara taught, Ramanuja insisted that he was only following the great Alavandar. Surprised by such an anachronistic claim, when Maladhara protested saying that Alavandar never taught Ramanuja, the redoubtable Ghoshti Purna himself endorsed Ramanuja's interpretation as authentic. When interrogated by Maladhara, Ramanuja quipped, 'Am I not the Ekalavya to Alavandar?' (suggesting that even as the tribal boy Ekalavya in the epic Mahabharata prayed before the image of the peerless teacher Drona and learnt archery through spiritual transmission by the sheer force of his dedication as a disciple, so had he, Ramanuja, absorbed the knowledge of Alavandar without ever learning from him directly). Finally, from Alavandar's son and disciple Tiruvarangap Perumal Araiyar, he learnt *charamopaya* or total reliance on the grace of the guru. Thus, in

Ramanuja's life there were 'five mediators' of Yamunacharya's teaching (Carman 1974: 40–1).

He was not only the spiritual guru but also the manager or *Senapati durantara* at the Srirangam temple (ibid.: 280). However, orthodox people became jealous of his rising prestige. There was even an attempt to poison him. Hence Ghoshti Purna directed Kidambi Achan to be his cook. A well-known Advaita scholar Yagnamurty, returning from Benares after vanquishing many pundits, heard of Ramanuja's popularity and came to Srirangam to challenge him to a debate on philosophical matters. The debate went on for sixteen days and Ramanuja seemed to be losing. After praying to the Lord, he received a divine message saying that he should go back to Yamunacharya's arguments refuting *mayavada* (doctrine of the illusoriness of the world). On the seventeeth day, Ramanuja walked in, confident and bright, and Yagnamurty felt like retreating. He conceded defeat and, in fact, became Ramanuja's disciple and was rechristened Emberumanar (after Ramanuja's own name).

Ramanuja undertook the customary yatra or religious tour of the country. He tried to replace the existing forms of worship by the *pancharatra* mode in places like the Anantapadmanabha Swami Temple in Trivandrum, Kerala, and Jagannath temple in Puri, Orissa, but met with resistance. In Tirupati, he established the temple once and for all as a Vaishnavite shrine and not both Saivite and Vaishnavite as it was long considered. He travelled to Kashmir with Kuresa, met the king, and got access to the *Bhodhayana Vritti*. He managed to read it with the help of the incisive Kuresa who is believed to have had a phenomenal memory. He defeated the pundits there in philosophical debates. It is said that Goddess Saraswati herself was so pleased with his erudition and personality that she conferred on him the title of *Bhashyakara* or commentator nonpareil.

He returned to Srirangam and resumed his mission. His followers requested him to write a decisive commentary on the scriptures to silence the Jains, the Buddhists, the Mayavadins, and others. Thus he started the monumental work *Sri Bhashya*. Kuresa was his scribe and Ramanuja gave him the liberty to stop writing whenever he did not agree with Ramanuja's interpretation. Kuresa's well-informed wife Andal Amma was also present during the composition. On one occasion Ramanuja was dictating the exegesis on the nature of self/

consciousness and expatiating upon Isvara or the Lord. He described the self as conscious of itself, saying that was its raison d'etre. Kuresa stopped writing and refused to proceed. Ramanuja was so incensed at this that he is said to have kicked the most incisive and endowed of his disciples. After a while, Ramanuja realized his error, that is he had departed from the Visishtadvaita doctrine that the self is not independent but is subservient and instead he had attributed self-sufficiency to the self in the manner of the Advaitic school. Hence Kuresa had persisted in protesting silently by refusing to proceed with his task of being the amanuensis. It is said that Ramanuja continued with his *Sri Bhashya* which, however, got disrupted by his exile to Karnataka. The *Ramanuja Divyasuri Charitai* says Ramanuja completed the work in 1155 after he returned from Melukote and that he died soon after.

From the time Ramanuja took over the management of the famed Srirangam temple, he brought in reforms in the administration after taking stock of the functioning of all departments, material as well as religious. Corrupt officials were sacked, his own disciples were put in charge of crucial departments. He also nominated a local chieftain Akalanganattalvan as supervisor. He tried to maintain a balance in the relationship between the Brahmin and non-Brahmin functionaries of the temple. He put his nephew and disciple Mudaliyandan in charge when he went on tour. Very soon, he began to face hostility from the temple community. He wanted to remove the chief priest Periya Koil Nambi, who was resisting his authority and was keeping the keys of the shrine himself, but Lord Ranganatha Himself appeared in Ramanuja's dream and directed him not to dislodge the high priest because he was dear to Him. However, Kuresa deployed a stratagem to bring round the chief priest. Once he was invited by the high priest to act as the ritual Brahmin guest on the eleventh day of the priest's mother's obsequies. His mother, when alive, had liked Kuresa's singing of the Tamil hymns. Hence Periya Koil Nambi, although an Advaitin, thought of gratifying his mother's soul by giving the honour to Kuresa during the ceremony. As is the custom, at the end of the feast, the *karta* or doer of the obsequies should offer gifts to the guest and ask ritualistically 'Are you satisfied?' and the latter should say 'Satisfied' (*triptosmi*). When, on this occasion, the priest uttered this ritual question, Kuresa kept silent. The priest sought to know what he wanted. 'The keys', came the cryptic reply. The priest was trapped by the ritual situation and handed the temple keys to Kuresa along with many other gifts. Kuresa threw away all the gifts and promptly handed over the keys to Ramanuja. Ramanuja was very pleased with Kuresa's intelligence as well as detachment and devotion. However, all this caused much animosity in the temple community. So much so that Ramanuja himself had to leave Srirangam and stay in a place called Tiruvellarai for two years until they sent the Araiyar to meet Ramanuja and invite him back to the temple and Ramanuja obliged.

Not only the temple community, but also the orthodox Brahmins in Srirangam's lay population had reason to resent Ramanuja's ascendancy and, especially, his ways. He moved freely among the people without minding caste taboos; he patronized his non-Brahmin disciples and cherished their devotion. He respected the women devotees in his mutt. He chided his Brahmin disciples for being so worldly while praising Urangavilli and Ponnachi, his non-Brahmin disciples, for being spiritually inclined. He supported Maha Purna ministering to the Panchama disciple of Alavandar, Maraner Nambi, during the latter's illness. He came to accept Maha Purna giving a Brahmin funeral to Maraner Nambi. What intrigued many was that while going to the Kaveri river for his bath, he would lean on the purest of his Brahmin disciples, Kuresa, but after bathing, he would put his hand on the bare shoulder of Urangavilli, the non-Brahmin devotee, to support himself. He freely gave Sri Vaishnava initiation (*samskara*s) to men and women from all castes. Thus an unorthodox Sri Vaishnava community grew in number. Naturally, Ramanuja's policies and activities provoked discontent and positive animus among those whose interests were injured in some way or the other. One Naluran, once a disciple of Kuresa, whose family was now deprived of certain hereditary privileges they had enjoyed in the temple, was so incensed at the doings of Ramanuja that he instigated the reigning Chola king to crack the whip against Ramanuja and his followers. When the soldiers went to the mutt to apprehend the acharya, Kuresa cleverly arranged to have Ramanuja escape without fully informing him of the situation and presented himself as the pontiff. He was taken to the king's court at Gangaikondacholapuram and the aged Maha Purna also accompanied him.

The Chola king asked Kuresa to subscribe to the statement that there was no god higher than Siva. Since Kuresa was a staunch Vaishnavite, he bluntly refused. He argued with the king, citing many scriptural and scholarly sources. When finally compelled, the clever Kuresa wrote that 'dronam is bigger than Siva', dronam and Siva being two units of measurement. The king's anger knew no bounds when outwitted, and he ordered that the eyes of the two dissenters be plucked out. One version of the event says, the soldiers plucked out the eyes of both the Sri Vaishnavas and left them outside. Another version says that Kuresa retorted saying that he would not allow his eyes to see sinners any more and plucked them out himself. On their way back, the aged Maha Purna breathed his last and Kuresa returned to Srirangam. It is said that he soon had to move to Tirumalirunjolai near Madurai because the atmosphere at Srirangam was not conducive.

In the meanwhile Ramanuja had fled from Srirangam along with a few devout disciples and followers, wearing lay clothes. They travelled west and reached the Nilgiri forests. They met some kindly hunters who claimed to be disciples of one Nallan Chakravarti, who was himself a devotee of Ramanuja and had done much for the poor and the outcastes. They were only too happy to help Ramanuja escape into Karnataka through the Kongu region. His fame had already reached that region because there was a woman called Kongu Piratti who had stayed sometime earlier in Srirangam and had *mantradiksha* or lay initiation from Ramanuja himself. She became his hostess for a few days. He was soon led by the tribals and hunters to interior Karnataka. He first reached the villages of Mirle and Saligramam and met with hostility from the local Jain population. He, therefore, moved to Tondanur which was then known as Yadavapura. He stayed in an old Yoga Narasimha temple. The place was the capital outpost of the Hoysala king Vittala Deva who was said to be a Jain by persuasion. The king had a daughter who was possessed by a spirit. The queen was anxious to get her cured. She heard from a pious Vaishnavite, Tondanur Nambi, about the spiritual power of the newly arrived acharya. Tondanur Nambi persuaded Ramanuja to go to the palace to meet the royal family though Ramanuja himself was reluctant, as an ascetic, to do this. Nambi thought it would be a helpful strategy to spread the Sri Vaishnava faith. The king was in a dilemma over inviting the acharya to his place because of the hostility of the Jains led by their guru. The queen thought of inviting the Jain priests to a feast to appease them. They turned down the invitation because the king had had one of his fingers cut off by the conquering 'Turkish Sultan' as a mark of his subservience and hence it was inauspicious for the Jains to attend the royal feast. The queen used this opportunity and persuaded her consort to invite the Vaishnava acharya since the Jain guru himself had failed to cure the princess. Ramanuja succeeded in exorcizing the spirit that possessed the girl and converted the king from a Jain to a Vaishnava and gave him the name Vishnuvardhana. The king, out of gratitude, rendered royal support to the acharya in renovating the temple and pond at Tondanur.

During his stay in Tondanur, the acharya felt an acute need for the fine white clay with which Sri Vaishnavites mark their body with vertical lines. The Lord appeared in his dream and directed him to go to Yadugiri hill where he would find the clay as well as discover an old temple covered over with tulsi or basil plants sacred to Lord Krishna. With the help of the outcaste devotees, Ramanuja got the outgrowth cleared and the gold ornaments of the deities and eventually the deities themselves surfaced. Ramanuja was so touched by the selfless service rendered by the outcastes that he gave them the name *'Tirukkulattar'* or the clan of Goddess Lakshmi. He declared that henceforth they should not be called *'Paraiyas'* and that they should be given the right to enter the temple on stated days, bathe in the sacred pond, and offer prayers. This was one of the most daring social reforms in the history of Hindu social organization by any pontiff. Ramanuja, under the royal patronage of King Vishnuvardhana, got the Tirunarayana temple renovated and the place came to be called Melukote because it was on a hilltop. A ruined place was brought back to life and it later emerged as a renowned centre of Sri Vaishnavism during the period from the twelfth to fifteenth century.

In the meanwhile, the acharya thought that the temple required a processional idol for festival seasons and it was said that the Sampat Kumara idol from the temple had been taken away by the invading Turkish troops along with many other treasures. In his ripe old age, Ramanuja undertook an arduous journey all the way to Delhi, met the Sultan, and found the lovely idol in the possession of the Sultan's sister, a young Turkish girl. Ramanuja managed to secure the idol from her. Legend has it that in the harem, when Ramanuja called out to the idol as *Chellapillai* or darling boy, it jumped down from the lap of the princess who was fondling it and came and sat on the venerable acharya's lap. The Turkish Sultan was convinced of Ramanuja's earnestness and allowed him to take away the idol. The girl also followed the idol. On the way, Ramanuja's group was attacked by dacoits but was saved by the forest tribals and outcastes. Ramanuja, therefore, came to cherish even more those people living outside of the Hindu varna or caste system. When he returned to Melukote with the Sampat Kumara idol, the temple festivities were marked by the freedom given to the Panchamas and outcastes to worship the deity.

Ramanuja established Vaishnava and Tamil traditions of worship in the temples of Karnataka, nominated fifty-two (*Aimbattiruvar*) disciples as heads to supervise various activities, arranged for the Azhwars' hymns to be recited, and legalized the rights of the outcastes to worship in the temple. Thus he strove to create an egalitarian society on enlightened principles.

In the meanwhile, things started changing for the better at Srirangam, which the acharya had left nearly eleven years earlier. News reached that the Chola king who had persecuted Ramanuja and the Sri Vaishnavites, had developed a carbuncle in the neck and eventually died after much suffering. The acharya also came to know of the fates of his dear Kuresa and much respected Maha Purna. He decided to get back to Srirangam, now that times were propitious. He left Melukote and returned to Srirangam and re-established his supremacy and the pontificate. The successor to the Chola throne also came and craved forgiveness for his father's sins and offered service and patronage. Ramanuja was reunited with Kuresa who was living at Tirumalirunjolai near Madurai during his master's exile in Karnataka. Ramanuja undertook a holy tour of the southern shrines of Azhwars as well as Tirupati. He arranged for his disciples to execute specific tasks and spread Sri Vaishnava thought and forms of worship. He also finished, it is said, his monumental *Sri Bhashya* and very soon after that attained liberation at the ripe age of 120.

History and Hagiography

J.B. Carman, in what is considered to be one of the most incisive books on Ramanuja, observes that 'the question of the historical usefulness of the traditional biographies of the Sri Vaishnava saints and teachers is one that deserves far more attention than it has received' (Carman 1974: 16). He believes that these biographies contain a great deal of material of historical value, especially in illuminating the social context of Ramanuja's life and the religious and social significance of his work as the leader of the Sri Vaishnava community in the late eleventh and early twelfth centuries (ibid.: 16–17).

It are the historical details of the acharya's life and personality that give so much tangibility to the legends about his progressive outlook, liberal spirit, and administrative and organizational abilities. However, the historical information is not without problems. The historian M.S. Govindasamy says, 'The date of Ramanujar requires a serious consideration on account of much controversy' (Endowment Lecture 2002:14; JTS:107). The hagiographic account of the fourteenth century, *Guruparamparai Prabhavam* mentions the term *'dhir labdha'*, according to which the year of Ramanuja's birth was *Pingala*, Saka era 939, the month *Chaitra*, and the *tithi Panchami*, the *paksha, Suklapaksha*, and the star *Tiruvadirai* (GPP 6000: 148). The narratives in the modes of both biography and hagiography hold that the Acharya was born in 1017 (Saka Era 939). Accordingly, the 'chronograms'—*dhirlabdha* and *dharmonashta*—were fixed as 1017 and 1137, respectively. Following this frame of reference, traditionally it is claimed that Ramanuja studied with the Advaita teacher Yadava Prakasa from 1033, entered Srirangam to see Alavandar in 1042, and took holy orders in 1049. He fled to Mysore five decades later in 1096, installed the Deity at Melukote in 1100, and returned to Srirangam in 1118. He died in 1137, thus living for an eventful and phenomenally long span of 120 years.

However, both epigraphists and historians have deep problems with this chronology, mainly because the Chola and Karnataka phases of his life point to a slightly later time. Above all, there is the vexed question of who the Chola king was who 'persecuted' Ramanuja. B.R. Gopal, the epigraphist, distinguishes between literary and epigraphical sources. The latter are documents recording an event of significance like a gift made, a tank excavated, or temple consecrated by kings and chieftains; they also contain details about local self-governing bodies or private individuals. Of the Karnataka inscriptions, he cites only one which directly reflected the religious and social conditions of the times, that is the Sravanabelagola inscription of Bukkaraya which refers to the conflict between the Jains and the Sri Vaishnavas and the award made by the then king (Gopal 1983:3). However, as an epigraphist he points out that such inscriptions are few. It is the later ones, from the late twelfth century onwards, which throw light on not only Ramanuja's sojourn in Karnataka but also the impact of his teaching as could be seen in the temple worship of the Sri Vaishnavas (ibid.: 4). There are, on the other hand, what he calls 'literary sources' which reconstruct the life of Ramanuja. We have a few of them figuring prominently in all discussions. *Divyasuri Charita* of Garuda Vahana Pandita, perhaps a contemporary of Ramanuja's, is considered the earliest. Then we have the hagiographic *Guruparamparai Prabhavam*, that is the glory of the line of preceptors type of narrative. As J.B. Carman and M.S. Govindasamy have noted, we have variations of them. The *Guruparamparai Prabhavam 6000* by Pinpalagiya Perumal Jiyar (பின் பழகிய பெரிய ஜியர்) is written in the style of medieval Tamil called Manipravala. It is cryptic and fast paced; it is a brief about the Karnataka period of Ramanuja's life. There are other literary sources like *Ramanuja Divyacharitram* in Tamil by Pillai Lokan Jiyar. Another *Guruparamparai Prabhavam* was by the third pontiff of the Parakala Mutt in Karnataka, Brahmatantra Svatantra Jiyar, and it is considered a *Vadagalai* (northern) version. As Carman points out, two hundred years after Ramanuja, the Sri Vaishnava tradition split into two, the northern and the southern schools (Carman 1974: 14). M.S. Govindasamy points out that the later acharya and commentator of the fourteenth century, Vedanta Desika, the most respected of Sri Vaishnava preceptors, mentions only the month and star of Ramanuja's birth, but no year, in his *Prabanda Saram*. A Sri Vaishnava researcher with the slant of a historian of modern times, S. Kalyanarama Iyengar, in his *Sri Ramanuja Charita Araichi Mahimai* (1978), is of the opinion that Ramanuja was born not on a Friday but on a Thursday. Several eminent historians have racked their brains over the discrepancies between the Chola inscriptions, the hagiographies, the Mysore inscriptions, and the literary narratives, some of which completely missed the mark, and hazarded some conclusions. The earliest English biographer Alkondavilli Govindacharya (1906) followed the traditional chronograms and tried to find corroborations in Rice's *Mysore Gazetteer*, *Indian Antiquaries*, *Epigraphia Carnatica* of earlier editions. However, T.A. Gopinatha Rao in 1917, while accepting the traditional dates, considered Kulothunga Chola I to be the persecutor (cited in ibid.: 45; Gopal 1983: 4, 9). Since he died in 1117, Ramanuja's period of exile from Tamil Nadu was constructed as 1079–1126. But that did not tally with the information in *Ramanuja Divya Charitai* that the *Sri Bhashya* was completed in 1155–6. This certainly threw into doubt the theory that Ramanuja died in 1137. However, another historian Sadasiva Pandarathar categorically rejected the surmise citing the king's official paean or *mei kirthi* which compares him to Vishnu. There were also grants made by Kulothunga I for recitation of Vaishnava hymns (MSG 2002: 8; JTS:103). M.S. Govindasamy rejected any anti-Vaishnavite theory, blaming internecine squabbles as having been solely responsible for Ramanuja's exile. While it is almost certain that Ramanuja lived through three Chola kings' rules—Carman mentions that it was five—the later events in his life do not tally with the reign of Kulothunga I. The renowned historian K.A. Nilakanta Sastri (*The Colas* 1950) argued that Kulothunga was a generic name for the 'Cola' king and the incident of the original Govindaraja idol being thrown into the sea from Chidambaram temple is attributed to Kulothunga II (whose regnal years happen to be 1135 to 1150), and is mentioned by his own teacher-poet Ottakkoottan in his *Ulas* and also in his *Takkayagabarani*. But the events of Ramanuja's life do not match with this. Hence Sastri suggested that the 'Chola' king could have been the short-lived Adhirajendra or Virarajendra, who ruled before Kulothunga I came to power (Gopal 1983: 8). However, even this is not quite satisfactory. T.N. Subramanian, who was the Madras Government epigraphist ('A Note on the Date of Ramanuja'), cited three Tamil verses mentioned in *Ramanuja Divya Charitai* which said that the *Sri Bhashya* was completed in 1155–6, that Ramanuja, who had left Srirangam in 1137–8, returned eleven years later and that Kuresa had to retreat during that period to Tirumalinnjolai. Therefore, T.N. Subramanian identified the persecuting Chola king as Kulothunga II whom he described as a fanatic (cited in Carman 1974: 45; Gopal 1983: 6). Historians, however, argue that although there is sufficient evidence to prove that Kulothunga II removed the Vishnu idol from the Chidambaram temple and courted the discontent of Vaishnavites, he was not at all opposed to Vaishnavism or Ramanuja; in fact, he gave grants to the Tirukkoyilur Vishnu temple (MSG 2002: 9; JTS:104) and his *mei kirthi* or official paean speaks of his respect for Vishnu. Hence, neither Kulothunga I nor Kulothunga II could have been the persecutor of Ramanuja. M.S. Govindasamy, therefore, considers that no political pressure would have caused Ramanuja's exile but only 'the strong dislike of orthodox Vaishnavites towards Ramanujar and dissatisfied functionaries of Srirangam temple' (MSG 2002:11; JTS:105) who must have plotted to dislodge Ramanuja. This historian even interprets the *mei kirthi* of Rajaraja II, the son and successor of Kulothunga II, in such a way as to conclude that Ramanuja was received honourably by the successor of Kulothunga II when he returned to Srirangam and was offered all patronage. The phrase '*Vilunta arisamayameduttu*' (MSG 2002: 12; JTS: 106) in the *mei kirthi* or the eulogy means restoring the fallen or weakened Vaishnavism and it alludes not to any Chola king's designs against Ramanuja but to the internal disturbance in the Vaishnava order at Srirangam (MSG 2002: 12; JTS: 105). He even cites verse two of Amudanar's *Ramanuja Nutrandadi*, a panegyric on Ramanuja which says that Ramanuja ignored in disgust the religious rebels as '*Kaittanan tiya samayak kalakarai*' (ibid.). Carman also expresses surprise that Amudanar does not allude to any historical event in Ramanuja's life though he too lived long enough. M.S. Govindasamy argues that the Chidambaram incident was an isolated one and cannot be taken as representative of the religious situation during Kulothunga II's rule. He even says there was no worship at the shrine of Govindaraja till the sixteenth century, that is during the reign of Achuta Raya. Hence he concludes that the Chola persecution of Ramanuja was a myth created by later-day Vaishnava hagiographers to make light of the hostile reaction of the orthodox group to the activities of Ramanuja (MSG 2002: 13; JTS: 106). While part of this argument is convincing, it is still not clear why the hagiographers should malign the Chola rulers instead of exposing the true opponents of Ramanuja's faith. It is obvious that there was much mutual suspicion between Vaishnavites and Saivites in the medieval period. The biographer P. Sri (1964: 286–7) contends that there is definitely glee in Ottakkoothar's reference to the incident of the Vishnu idol being thrown into the sea which, in his opinion, connotes religious prejudice.

The Point of View of the Epigrapher

More than anything else, the supposed chronological details given by traditional narratives do not match the Karnataka inscriptions and evidence. It is agreed that Maha Purna died in 1138 and that by that time Ramanuja had already fled to Karnataka. Traditional accounts say that Ramanuja followed the river Kaveri as far as Ramanathapuri, also known as Vahnipushkarani (GPP 6000: 246), then proceeded to Tonnur via Mithila-Saligrama. These accounts also say that there was a tank in Tonnur at which Dasarathi was asked to be seated and the local people who came to the tank and touched the waters were all converted to Sri Vaishnavism. B.R. Gopal holds that this is not at all possible. However, there is a small shrine at Tonnur with Ramanuja's footprints and a holy fountain nearby where one Vaduga Nambi is supposed to have embraced the new faith. B.R. Gopal (1983: 11) thinks that traditional narratives are a mixture of fact and fiction, and feels that there must have been a compelling reason why Ramanuja abandoned his pontificate seat. There is evidence, although not direct, that he found in the Hoysala country a congenial atmosphere to propagate his faith and made Tondanur, and later Melukote, centres of his activity. Mirle and Saligrama each have a Yoganarasimha temple associated with Ramanuja; so do Tondanur and Melukote. Gopal refers to two epigraphs at Mirle and Saligrama, of the thirteenth and fourteenth centuries. The one dated 19 August 1299 records a grant by an individual for lighting a lamp that would burn perennially in the Narasimha temple. This suggests that, possibly as a consequence of the Sri Vaishnava movement in Karnataka after Ramanuja's coming over to this part of the country, Mirle must have become a Sri Vaishnava centre. Carman too notes that although there is no direct evidence of Ramanuja's influence, Jain influence declined in Karnataka with the ascendancy of Sri Vaishnavism which can only be attributed to Ramanuja's decade-long efforts. B.R. Gopal cites more solid evidence at Saligrama—a temple built for Sri Ramanuja, the objects worshipped there being the footprints of Ramanuja on a high pedestal and images of eight of his disciples. In front of the temple is 'a pond containing water in which the feet of Ramanuja were once washed' (Mysore Archaeological Report 1913:16). On the beam of the doorway to the pond is a damaged epigraph which refers to 'Embar', 'Andan', and 'Achan' (Govinda, Dasarathi, and Kadambi Achan) of

Srirangam mutt who granted some privileges to the Sri Vaishnavas of 'Saligava', that is Saligrama. These must have been new converts. This record, according to B.R. Gopal (1983: 13), 'provides indirect corroborative evidence to the legendary account of Ramanuja's visit to Saligrama'.

Ramanuja's next stop was Tonnur in Mandya region where he is said to have cured the daughter of King Vishnuvardhana. It was the capital of the Hoysalas in 1127. The name Tondanur appears in the records of the twelfth century and more frequently in those of the thirteenth century, points out B.R. Gopal. Discounting the conversion story entirely, he refers to several inscriptions that show that the king was a liberal who patronized all faiths and that there is no evidence to prove that he was a Jain by faith. The Tonnur inscriptions throw light on the role of the disciples of Sri Ramanuja in propagating the faith through such acts as temple building and instituting new services (Gopal 1983: 16). B.R. Gopal thinks that this sort of discipline was instituted to inject fresh vigour into the already existing Vishnu worship in Karnataka and 'through it underline the prominence of *saranagati* and *prapatti* which Ramanuja propagated' (ibid.: 16). In this connection, B.R. Gopal considers the copper plate of Krishnaraja Wodeyar II of Mysore preserved in the Krishna temple at Tonnur to be the most eloquent testimony of Ramanuja's influence. It registers the strong tradition of Sri Ramanuja's stay at Tonnur. The king found that within his own kingdom, the best and most suitable place for the residence of Sri Vaishnavas was Yadavapura. Yadavapura, ruled by Vishnuvardhana, is described as having become sanctified by Sri Ramanuja. 'This could be considered as an epigraphical evidence, though very late, confirming the traditional account of Sri Ramanuja's visit to Tonnur' (ibid.: 16). The Yoganarasimha temple at Tonnur has Tamil records about gifts of items and food offerings. The 'donatrix' might have been Tamil. One of the records refers to one Tiruvarangadasa who lived up to the end of 1174, and was possibly the force behind these temples of Yoganarasimha, Lakshmi Narayana, and Krishna. Many of the donors to the temple hailed from Tamil Nadu and were all Sri Vaishnavites; some were local people who had turned Sri Vaishnavites (ibid.: 20). Interestingly, some purchased land at Tonnur and granted it to Kanchi Varadaraja temple. The language and vocabulary of the Sri Vaishnava temple services enunciated by

Ramanuja are found in some of these records, for example *tiruvaradhana* (ritualized worship of the deity). A profound influence was seen in according Tamil Prabandhas a prominent place in Karnataka temples too (ibid.: 21), especially *Tiruvaymozhi* of Nammazhwar. In 1181 at Tonnur, a Tiruvarangadasa is described as a reciter of *Tiruvaymozhi*. In 1186 a grant of land for food offering is made on the occasion of a special festival to highlight the glory of the hymns.

Architecturally, too, the Yoganarasimha temple underwent a good deal of renovation. The sanctum is a simple structure of Hoysala-Dravidian styles tending more towards the latter (ibid.: 21). Interestingly, in the Lakshmi Narayana temple, the deity called Nambinarayana is a standing image of six feet, resembling the deity in the Narayana temple at Melukote. The style is more Dravidian than Hoysala (ibid.: 23). B.R. Gopal concludes that the Yoganarasimha temple must have come into existence earlier than 1136 and the acharya must have come to Karnataka in 1138 and taken his abode there. It is likely that the Lakshmi Narayana temple was built when the acharya was in Tonnur. Maybe he stayed for about six years in Tonnur (from 1138 to 1144–5) and moved to Melukote and stayed there for another five years (1145–50) (ibid.: 23).

As for Melukote, the earliest record is a twelfth century one about some service to God Narayana of Yadavagiri by an individual. The Tirunarayana temple or Chelapileraya temple at Melukote was built over the years from the Hoysalas to the Wodeyars of the eighteenth and nineteenth centuries. The style is early Hoysala. Did Ramanuja move to Melukote from Tonnur for the sake of *tiruman*, that is fine white clay? As an epigrapher Gopal notes how this legend gained ground and got accepted even by the beginning of fourteenth century. He cites inscription No. 25 dated 1319 on a slab in the Garuda shrine stating that Madappa-dannayaka, son of Perumaludeva-dannayaka, made over to the temple the title of the land originally noticed by Emberumanar (that is Ramanuja) for tiruman. Even today the clay is exported from the place. But B.R. Gopal thinks that probably the Hoysala officer Surigaya Nagayya and even the king prevailed upon the acharya to move to Melukote to participate in the consecration of the temple. Vishnuvardhana was becoming politically strong. He had even crossed the Tungabadra river and occupied Chalukya territory. Thus the atmosphere was congenial for the acharya to propagate his faith. Sri Vedantadesika, the saint-poet of the fourteenth century, describes Melukote as the *Vijayasthana* (seat of victory) of Ramanuja. What was the victory that the acharya achieved? Melukote emerged as a great Sri Vaishnava centre during the period of Ramanuja's stay there. Indirect testimony is found in 1544 in the *prakara* (outer corridor) of the Narayana temple. It refers to the seal to be used by the Yathirajamatha and states that it was the place where the *Bhashyakara* (Ramanuja) had once stayed (*Sri Bhashyakararu bijayamadi idda Etiraja-matha*). This fact had lingered on for four centuries before it came to be recorded in this epigraph. It is to be understood that the mutt was later built where *Yatiraja* (Ramanuja) once stayed. However, by 1256 a shrine for Sri Ramanuja had been built at Melukote called *Bhashyakara Sannidhi* besides a *Ramanuja Kuta* (rest house) for pilgrims. These are the only near contemporary records as evidence of Ramanuja's sojourn in Karnataka (Gopal 1983: 26). He finds, however, no historical basis for Ramanuja's visit to Delhi from Melukote and notes that this period was one of great confusion in the north and there was no stable government. However, Melukote, after Ramanuja's return to Srirangam, began to receive patronage from the rulers of the Vijayanagara kingdom. One notices the use of hagiographic language in the descriptions eulogizing the acharya. In 1556 a grant is made for offerings to the image of the acharya consecrated at his birthplace Sriperumpudur (ibid.: 27). Sri Vedantadesika describes Yadavagiri as the ear-ornament of Karnataka in his *Sankalpasuryodaya*. In 1369 a Bukkaraya I epigraphic record mentions land for prayer offerings for the Nammazhwar festival of twenty days. The last ten days (*Raapathu*) were meant for the recital of *Tiruvaymozhi* (this is reminiscent of the custom in Srirangam and other Vishnu temples in Tamil Nadu). There are numerous records of the establishment of a '*desantara matha*' (choultry or inn), Ramanuja Kuta to feed Vaishnavas. It is interesting to find some records mentioning dishes which are special to Sri Vaishnava temples, for example '*akkola payasu*' which is '*akkaravadisal*' (1528), and '*Atirasa*' to Lord Narasimha (sixteenth century). Another set of records of 1519–85 refers to '*Senabova* Ramanuja', probably an officer of the mutt. Three records of Achutadevaraya (1534–5) give details of food to be offered to the God and one finds the typical Sri Vaishnava term 'amudu' (food) added to all dishes—*paruppu amudu*, *kariamudu*, and even *churul amudu* (betel leaf offered at the end of the ritual offering) (ibid.: 32). More than half a dozen records in the temple belong to the reign of Sadasivaraya in the sixteenth century. One of these makes a gift of land to Vedanti Ramanuja jiya described as '*Ubhaya Vedantacharya*'. The donor belonged to the Nandyala family. Further records of 1574 show arrangements made for reciting *Yati raja-satpadi*, the work in praise of Ramanuja by Sri Vedantadesika. Similarly arrangements were made for reciting Ramanuja's own *Sri Bhashya*. From the fourteenth to the sixteenth century under Vijayanagara rule, new types of services were instituted (ibid.: 36) including the reciting of the 4000 prabandhas in Tamil. Within the temple, shrines for Ramanuja, Nammazhwar, and later Pillai Lokacharya, a separate shrine for Vedantadesika came up. The inscriptions at Tonnur are almost all in Tamil. Quite a number of Sri Vaishnavas from Tamil Nadu moved into Karnataka in Sri Ramanuja's wake. The impact of the Tamil language was conspicuous. In the Vijayanagara period, the epigraphic language was Kannada, but several Tamil terms entered, for example *amisai* (food offering) and *kari amudu* (cooked vegetables) (ibid.: 37). Such records are of linguistic interest. The temple of Melukote itself was now under the control of the 'Fifty-two' (அம்பத்திருவர்) Sri Vaishnavas, left behind by Ramanuja. This body emerged as the most powerful custodian of temple property. Under Wodeyar II, a number of grants were made. A record of Tipu Sultan also reveals the continued patronage to the temple at Melukote. Several scholars in the Veda, in astrology, in grammar, etc. received gifts of lands. Such learned Vaishnavas were invited to settle down at Yadugiri. In 1785 an epigraph of Tipu Sultan (No. 56) records a gift of male and female elephants to the temples of Tirunarayana and Narasimha. Melukote now had two managers: one Hindu and one Muslim. But there is no reference to the 'Fifty-two' which suggests that the line of disciples was no longer administering the temple (ibid.: 39).

What do we make of all these narratives in our endeavour to understand the chronology of acharya Ramanuja? It is most likely that he was born in 1077 and Bittaladevan alias Vishnu Vardhana ruled between 1111 and 1141. Ramanuja spent about eleven years between 1138 and 1150 in the Karnataka region. He must have returned to Srirangam by 1150, completed the *Sri Bhashya*, evidently with the help of Kuresa, despite his blindness, and breathed his last by 1155–6. That means, he might not have lived for 120 years as legends claim. But he had seen and done much, despite the twenty years counted out, to lessen animosity and ignorance among human beings by turning their minds to the supreme holder of all primal virtues, Lord Vishnu.

The Place of Ramanuja in Indian Thought and Cultural History

Ramanuja was certainly not the founder of Vaishnavism. There was Vaishnavism before Ramanuja. This is precisely what Ramanuja himself tirelessly stressed. He pointed out that he followed in a line of great acharyas who propounded Vaishnava thought known in the Tamil country, such as Alavandar (meaning one who came to rule) and before him the venerable Nathamuni who was Alavandar's grandfather. In between, there had been a few devoted disciples who had sustained this faith and handed it over to Alavandar. The *Guruparamparai Prabhavam* traces the line of transmission from Nathamuni to Uyyakkondar to Manakkal Nambi to Alavandar (GPP 6000: 171). They nurtured the legacy of Nathamuni. Alavandar himself had an impressive array of devoted disciples, Sri Saila Purna (Periya Tirumalai Nambi), Thiruvarangattu Araiyar, Maha Purna (Periya Nambi), Ghoshti Purna (Tirukkottiyur Nambi), Kanchi Purna (Tirukkacchi Nambi) and Maladhara.

In turn, Alavandar was looking for a worthy successor to himself and there is reason to believe that he heard about Ramanuja as a young and ardent scholar learning under Yadava Prakasa, the renowned teacher of Advaita of the Bhedabheda school at Kanchipuram. Thus Alavandar was Ramanuja's *paramaguru* and Nathamuni his *parameshtiguru*. The self-consciousness with which these acharyas identified their location in traditional Vaishnavism that was being constructed by going back to the mystic poets called the Azhwars who had sung the hymns called *pasurams* and the goals they set for themselves, are testimony enough to the making of an alternative philosophical and religious tradition to the ruling Advaita. The Indian philosophical tradition is often made synonymous with the school of Advaita which rejected the separate existence of anything other than the Brahman which is one's own self. Culturally speaking, Sankara's triumphs over Buddhists and Mimamsakas helped to establish his ideology as the dominant one governing the Hindu way of life.

However, as Swami Vivekananda in his paper 'Historical Evolution of India' pointed out, the high intellectuality of the movement of Sankara was of little service to the masses, 'because of its strict adherence to caste laws, very small scope for ordinary emotion and making Sanskrit the only vehicle of communication'. He went on to say, 'Ramanuja, on the other hand, with a most practical philosophy, a great appeal to the emotions, an entire denial of birthrights before spiritual attainments and appeals through popular tongue, completely succeeded in bringing the masses back to the Vedic religion' (quoted in Swami Ramakrishnananda 1899 [1959: Preface]). Until as late as the twentieth century, for western scholars Hinduism invariably meant Sankara's thinking. It is only recently that scholars have started taking interest in Ramanuja's thought.[2] There was even some contempt in the distinction that was made between Sankara as a metaphysician and Ramanuja as a theologian. When we go back to Ramanuja's time, we can see how he was trying to steer clear of the dominant groups and establish an alternative mode of relating the self to reality. He cited the experiential attestations of a number of mystical seekers who had found their refuge in the Lord. In his famous work *The Wonder That was India* the modern-day Indologist A.L. Basham notes:

Ramanuja was not as brilliant a metaphysician as Sankara, but Indian religion perhaps owes even more to him than to his predecessor. In the centuries immediately following his death his ideas spread all over India, and were the starting point of most of the devotional sects of later times. (Basham 1954: 335)

Ramanuja was thus able to conceive of and construct an alternative system of thought which came to be called Visishtadvaita. As Narasimhachary puts it, 'Religion without a philosophical basis becomes superstition and philosophy without a religious background becomes dry metaphysics. Ramanuja's system provides a happy blend of these two important dimensions of man's spiritual life' (Narasimhachary 2004: 13). Traditional accounts say that when Ramanuja visited the court of the king of Kashmir, he traced the Visishtadvaita[3] interpretation of the *Brahmasutra* of Vyasa to an ancient text called *Bodhayanavritti*. He also referred chiefly to the commentaries and glossing by Tanka, Dramida, Guhadeva, Kapardi, and Bharuchi (AKVG 1906 [2004: 120]). Ramanuja identified himself with these preceptors who could be called 'purvacharyas' or teachers of remote antiquity (Yamunacharya 1988: 2). Immediately after his time, the newly formed community needed to affirm its authority in the society. Hence the proliferation of narratives on Ramanuja's life and feats. Hence also the attempts to draw the line of Azhwars and acharyas which would facilitate a sense of continuity.

Ramanuja as an acharya brought a reorientation to the ancient Vaidiki religion which came to be designated as Hinduism. Its scriptures, the Vedas, were in two parts. The first one constituted the *Karmakanda* portion which prescribed certain elaborate and expensive fire sacrifices called yagnas and *homas* led by the priestly class of Brahmins. It was also the Vaidiki society which conceived of the varna system or caste hierarchy. Ramanuja himself hailed from an erudite Vaidiki family called the *Somayaji* clan, the name implying the performance of certain highly specialized yagnas or ritual fire sacrifices. There was also the other side to the Vedas, the second part, in which searching questions were asked about the nature of ultimate reality (Brahman), the relation between self and the phenomenal universe and the mode of knowing. This has been described as Vedanta, that is the end of Veda as embedded in the Upanishads. All acharyas have sought to pay attention to interpreting the *mahavakyas* or the canonical utterances of the Upanishads, each according to his *darsana* (philosophy) and experiential knowledge. Hence this portion of the Vedas is known as *Gnanakanda*, that is the part discussing the attainment of self-knowledge. The restrictions on who can be initiated into *Brahmagnana* or the knowledge of the ultimate reality were strictly followed. The Brahmins had the sole privilege of being ritually initiated into the system. Each of the castes in the hierarchy had certain demarcated lines of activity that could not be transgressed. This rigid social system was preserved and exceptions were made only when the case was beyond all social and cultural obligations.

It is in this context that Ramanuja's role as a social reformer should be located and analysed.[4] It has been held by admirers of Ramanuja that he transcended all social barriers of caste and class and proclaimed the essentialism of the spirit.[5] In the hagiographies, too, certain episodes have been tirelessly reiterated to extol his social consciousness. For example, when he was sent out of the school of Yadava Prakasa and when Alavandar also died without initiating

Ramanuja as his successor, he turned to Tirukkacchi Nambi who was a *Vaisya* (belonging to the merchant class and, therefore, below the Brahmin in rank) and requested him to accept him as his disciple. Tirukkacchi Nambi protested saying that it would amount to violating the code enjoined on each caste in the hierarchy. As a guru, he might have to receive certain offerings which might entail physical gestures of obeisance such as prostrating before the teacher. Hence Tirukkacchi Nambi, although much revered as an intimate devotee of Lord Varadaraja of Kanchipuram, could not accept the suggestion that he be Ramanuja's acharya. M. Yamunacharaya in his biography (in the Bhavan series) remarks that Tirukkacchi Nambi offered to teach him whatever he could on the principle cited in *Bharadwaja Samhita* that yogis are born among all castes (Yamunacharya 1988:10–11). There are slight variations in the different narratives. In some, Ramanuja is said to have prostrated before Tirukkacchi Nambi. The English biographer Alkondavilli Govindacharya writes that Ramanuja admitted 'the legality and expediency of the caste system', yet felt it ought to be disregarded in special cases where such spiritually advanced souls as Kanchi Purna were concerned (AKVG 1906 [2004: Ch. X, 50]). This intriguing phrase 'legality and expediency of the caste system' calls for a deeper discussion.

Another signal instance of Ramanuja confronting socially challenging, sometimes embarrassing, situations relates to the last days of Maraner Nambi and, finally, his death. Alavandar spotted Maraner Nambi as a spiritually advanced soul and hence included him in the pantheon of his disciples. When Maraner Nambi took on the disease of his master out of sheer devotion, he suffered much and was ministered to by Maha Purna who brought him the *prasadam* (food offering) from the Srirangam temple. When he died, Maha Purna had no hesitation in cremating him according to the *Brahmamedha* rites which are accorded only to Brahmins. Ramanuja was embarrassed by the radical length to which his preceptor Maha Purna went in flagrantly violating caste codes. He protested to Maha Purna, worried about the social implications of such an act. There was a significant exchange between Maha Purna and Ramanuja in which the latter expressed the anxiety that while he was trying to keep the fence in shape and maintain social order, Maha Purna was doing away with the cultural fabric of the society: 'Sire, I am building a system, but you are pulling it down.' Maha Purna delivered a veritable sermon on the need for transcending caste. He said he was not for 'half-measures'. He reminds Ramanuja of the impressive line of exceptions in Hindu epic and puranic literature. 'Am I superior to Rama, the Hero of the Ikshvaku race? Is Maraner inferior to the bird Jatayu, for whom Rama performed the *brahmamedha*? Am I greater than Dharma Putra? Is Maraner lower than Vidura to whom the same *samskara* was administered?' (AKVG 1906 [2004: 144]). If Maha Purna is radical, Ramanuja is a reconciler par excellence. The *Guruparamparai Prabhavam* records a conversation which should be borne in mind by any latter-day discussant of Ramanuja's social ideology.[6] This will facilitate a nuanced understanding of Ramanuja's effort to handle caste issues.

Similarly, one must ponder the episode of Ramanuja sharing with all the people the inner import of the Ashtakshari mantra given to him by Ghoshti Purna or Tirukottiyyur Nambi. Surely this incident must have happened in the premises of the Tirukkottiyur temple. But, as J.B. Carman asks, who could have been the people in the congregation to whom Ramanuja expounded the significance of the mantra? Is it not likely that it was only to those who were allowed to enter the temple, implying that no outcaste would have been permitted to go into the temple in those days? When we try to equate what Ramanuja did on that occasion with modern attempts at establishing equality, we may be ignoring the limitations under which Ramanuja must have functioned. It is likely that devotees and believers would have listened to Ramanuja. Among them, not every one might have had the required preparation or what is called *adhikaram* to receive the mantra.[7] This does not mean that Ramanuja was not egalitarian. It does mean that his democratic venture to share secret scriptural knowledge with the common people was indeed a bold step forward. The event, however, was so appealing to the imagination of latter-day biographers and chroniclers that they presented a larger-than-life image of Ramanuja by hoisting him on the temple tower itself. It is probable that he ascended the second balcony of the inner *vimana* or the tower over the sanctum and called to the people. While it is fashionable to claim that Ramanuja was above distinctions, it is truer to say that he was one of the few acharyas hailing from the Vaidiki tradition to come into a social reality later in his life which demanded a reorientation of human relationships and a spiritual course. Here, in the Tirukkottiyur temple incident, he shows admirable enthusiasm as a young pontiff. This openness of mind certainly prepares him for the bold move to declare the outcastes to be Tirukkulattar meaning 'people belonging to the family of Lakshmi the Divine Mother', when in his old age he had to retrieve a sacred idol from the Turkish sultan and bring it to Melukote with the help of the pariahs. M. Narasimhachary in his recent biography cites Swami Vivekananda's acknowledging that the 'heavenly touch of the great Ramanuja converted the down-trodden pariahs into Alvars' (Narasimhachary 2004: 11). It may be remembered that it is the Bhakti movement that swept the Tamil country from the seventh century onwards which challenged caste supremacy in spiritual matters. Many of the Vaishnava Azhwars and Saiva Nayanmars (devotees of Vishnu and Siva respectively) came from different caste and class backgrounds. They also included women.

The experience of exile from his place of residence caused by religious and political circumstances of hostility makes Ramanuja an interesting subject of study. Exile and accommodation are critically interesting subjects for a modern reader. Ramanuja may be said to have established a diasporic community of Tamil Vaishnavites in the Mandya and Mysore regions as a result of his exile in Karnataka. Although there are glaring historical discrepancies regarding the vexed question of which Chola king actually persecuted the Vaishnavas and whether he persecuted them at all, or, for that matter, whether Ramanuja did really convert the Hoysala king Bittaladevan from Jainism, or whether Ramanuja went to meet the Delhi sultan all the way from Melukote, Ramanuja was certainly caught in a difficult situation when summoned to the court of the Chola king. That Kuresa and Maha Purna resolved to bear the brunt of the political pressure speaks volumes for their devotion to Ramanuja and no less to the cause of Vaishnavism. But does it appear somewhat selfish that Ramanuja should run away from the mutt leaving the two to face the persecution?

The historian M.S. Govindasamy, in his endowment lecture 'A Brief Historical Study of Sri Ramanujar' delivered at the University of Madras in 2002, raised this issue and went on to ask how a person of Ramanuja's compassionate nature could forget what was happening to his preceptor and disciple and be immersed in establishing a

Vaishnava community in an alien region and go about constructing temples and establishing mutts. He firmly believes that since all the narratives praise Ramanuja's humane qualities, he could not have been a callous person allowing others to suffer on his account. We, as modern readers, can perhaps surmise that those were days of poor communication and logistics and, anxious as Ramanuja must have been, as is evident from the account of how he sent a few of his disciples back to Srirangam on a reconnoitring trip, it could not have been easy for him to establish quick contact, not to speak of the day-to-day problem of fleeing though a dense forest into an unknown region. Certainly, Ramanuja had to deal with many unforeseen circumstances and forces, which must have been material, creaturely, existential, political, and philosophical. If his interaction either with Maraner Nambi or Tirukkacchi Nambi helped him take an enlightened view of caste relationships, one must remember that he was relating to two very senior men who were special for the Paramaguru Alavandar, the one being the 'master's man', the other, one of his prime disciples. There might not have been such an embarrassment in this relationship. In fact, he cherished Tirukkacchi Nambi and even adored him. However, the real challenge for Ramanuja must have come during his fleeing for his life, when the hunters in the Nilgiri forests came forward to guide him and his followers literally out of the woods. A high caste Brahmin would certainly have found it difficult or awkward to negotiate the public space given his ritualistic taboos regarding pollution. This is more so if the Brahmin happens to be the pontiff of an orthodox mutt. Ramanuja was, therefore, really in a situation that challenged his character and personality. He must have been touched by the hunters' regard for his well-being and safety and those of his followers. The biographies note that the hunters did not take any undue advantage of the situation or ask him to compromise. On the other hand, they were anxious to find a Brahmin in a nearby place who could feed the acharya. *Guruparamparai Prabhavam* says that they brought honey and millet'(GPP 6000: 242). As food items, these are not regarded as ritualistically polluted. No cooked food served by the hunters was eaten by the acharya and his men. In fact, he received hospitality from one Kongupiratti who was a Brahmin woman who had once received mantradiksha or initiation from Ramanuja at Srirangam. However, even now ultra-orthodox Brahmins would not take food cooked by women of other households especially on ritual occasions. When we remember all these factors, we are able to examine Ramanuja's predicament and openness with a greater degree of subtlety. As Ramanuja proceeds towards Mirle and Saligram near Sravanabelagola in the Karnataka region and eventually wins the confidence of King Vishnuvardhana as well as the local people at Tondanur, and later at Melukote, he once again settles down into a more established way of life. However, the mammoth effort to renovate the Melukote Tirunarayana temple calls for full-fledged physical help and cooperation from the lower caste people in removing the overgrowth and in re-establishing the temple as a living place of worship. It is this experience which refines his sense as a guru with a true egalitarian spirit and he opens the temple to those who helped him found it, albeit only on stated days. This may not be sufficiently reformist in the eyes of a modern reader. But considering the fact that such a move was simply not possible in those days of diehard orthodoxy, this is indeed a revolution. That a temple festival would become a carnival where the low and the high would mingle with each other is probably the earliest starting point of modern-day reorganization. This awareness of the rights and privileges of the suppressed majority in Hindu society must have prompted Ramanuja to name them Tirukkulattar. Legend has it that he had even greater occasion to be grateful to such people on the way from Delhi because the tribals saved his party and the holy idol from an attack by dacoits. Some secondary sources have been cited to show that this happened a little away from the Nagpur region and that as late as the nineteenth century, outcastes of the region had organized festivals calling themselves followers of Ramanuja. We may not be able to find accurate historical evidence corroborating Ramanuja's passing through this region in central India. But that he should have felt the need for recognizing the place of such people within society cannot be sweepingly dismissed. That the untouchables rendered 'yeoman' service in the old sense of the term, is acknowledged in all the narratives dealing with his sojourn in Karnataka. There is also recorded attestation that these people were given certain privileges of worship in the *Perumal* temples in Tonnur and Melukote.

Ramanuja seems to have shown the same social sensitivity in temple management too. When he assumed charge of the Srirangam temple, it was definitely no primrose path for the relatively young outsider. Even the *Guruparampara* and other narratives record the resistance of the traditional priestly class which enjoyed unchallenged privileges in the running of the temple complex. The biographer Kalyanarama Iyengar gives a detailed account of how Ramanuja tried to distribute the various tasks to different communities, often maintaining the status quo, but occasionally switching parties and castes. The account shows that he was cautious and did not want to make radical alterations. This seems to be a special feature of his personality. Carman notes that Ramanuja did manage to introduce new rules and new temple officers without permanently alienating the representatives of the previous regime. This meant not only a new cooperation between different Brahmin sub-castes but also between Brahmins and non-Brahmins in the temple administration (Carman 1974: 36). For example, he considered replacing a non-Brahmin with a Brahmin in temple administration in two cases as is recorded in the *Koilozhugu*. But in both, he decided to retain the non-Brahmin in the positions of temple accountant and of one who offered the coconut to the deity at the temple. Carman concludes that Ramanuja's temple management policy was more liberal than what had existed earlier and it is this 'relative liberalism' with reference to caste differences within the Sri Vaishnava community that is emphasized in a number of stories. He points out that this emphasis may have increased in the later Tengalai biographers (that is the southern subsect which gave a greater place to Tamil hymns and which canonized *prapatti* as the ultimate *upayam* or instrument for salvation). But such emphasis was minimal or even missing in the Vadagalai versions (that is the northern subsect) of the biographies. However, there are some unsavoury aspects to his attempts at reorganizing the temple management. The work *Koilozhugu* has been cited by all scholars of Ramanuja as reflecting the play of forces operating during that time. The signal instance of resistance, as we noted earlier, is that of the chief priest Amudhanar who was cleverly brought round by Kuresa to hand over the temple keys. Carman cites the oral tradition which has a different version of the events; the descendants of Amudhanar's family alleged that Ramanuja tried to poison him (Carman 1974: 35).[8] That Ramanuja had to go away from Srirangam and stay in a nearby town called Tiruvellarai for two years is recorded in the *Koilozhugu* (ibid.:

44–5) and it testifies to the hostility that he had to face. Kuresa too, after his blinding, had to retreat to Tirumalirunjolai near Madurai (GPP 6000: 261) until Ramanuja returned from Karnataka to Srirangam. These incidents show intra-religious conflicts and reveal Ramanuja in a very human light.

From all these predicaments mediated through different kinds of narration, often from sectarian perspectives, one can discern that Ramanuja must have been a truly historical figure endeavouring to handle varying situations touching upon social, cultural, and political realities. He did not evade them through metaphysics. It is in this light that we must place the Tamil play *Ramanujar*.

A Critique of the Play Ramanujar

Indira Parthasarathy was awarded the prestigious Saraswati Samman for the year 1999 by the K.K. Birla Foundation, Delhi, in 2001 for the play *Ramanujar* (1997). In his preface to the play, he states that he has made significant departures from the existing versions of the story of Ramanuja. Parthasarathy's play *Ramanujar* (1997) is a significant addition to the corpus of literature on Ramanuja. In one sense, we may say most of the narratives on Ramanuja have an *ur-*. In traditional scholarship, this is called source study. However, this source study cannot be simply a matter of tracing certain items to specific sources or the original context. The way the later texts draw from, handle, or problematize certain details make their relation to the source study critically interesting. In the case of the Ramanuja lore, traditionally a few works are listed as authentic sources, such as *Ramanuja Divya Charitam*, *Divya Suricharitham*, *Ethirajavaibhavam*, *Ramanuja Champu*, *Ethirajavamsathi*, *Guruparamparai Prabhavam*, and *Koilozhugu*. When we see the way certain episodes, *siddhantas*, or doctrines and ideas are reiterated, we become aware that every such narrative is an attempt to empower a group, a region, or a personality. Parthasarathy justifies the alterations he makes to the incidents in the sources on the basis of the kind of historical consciousness characteristic of the Indian mind. He points out that there have been several narratives exalting this great man but each one of them has been much enhanced by the subjective power of imagination of the writer whether he is a biographer, panegyrist, poet, or chronicler. In general, it is believed that the Indian consciousness does not have a historical sense and pays no attention to the temporal succession of events in its narration. This is the reason why genres like legends and hagiographies have enjoyed support and reputation among Indians. Although modernity has made a deep impact on our literature and has created cognates of western forms like the novel and realistic drama, there is the centuries-old orientation towards the fantastic and the mythical which does not die easily. The Indian mind tends to look for a certain presence of an eternal reality beneath terrestrial existence. Indira Parthasarathy is certainly not an essentialist but a self-conscious modernist with a striking social orientation in his thinking. His historical view is far from being monological. In fact, he refuses to trade in any softened or mythicized images of events, movements, personalities, and issues.

His great play *Nandan Kathai* (1976) is the most forceful example of his dialogic approach to history and myth. Usually, the story of Nandan is projected in the hagiographic mode exalting the element of *bhakti* which allowed murder to be projected as martyrdom. In presenting the pariah devotee of the dancing Nataraja, Indira Parthasarathy drastically moved away from the source narratives and read the received story against the grain. In a powerful use of the features of the theatre of menace and violence, Indira Parthasarathy in *Nandan Kathai* offered a clinical dissection of the caste Hindu society of the early middle ages. He spared none of the upper castes in his ruthless exposure of what is called Brahminism. With an almost savage glee, he turned a utopian story into a dystopia. His dramatic power of stichomythic dialogue, cryptic alliterative verse, and racy language accomplished an almost impossible feat which stunned many a pious reader. In the play *Ramanujar*, he attempts to read the life and personality of this medieaval Vaishnava acharya or preceptor in terms of their contemporary relevance. In fact, he states in his preface to the play that Ramanuja is our contemporary and that this is the awareness one should get while reading the play. The writer declares wittily that any intellectual who dared to dissent and think differently was in subsequent eras appropriated by the establishment, thus completely annulling his radicalism. Hence, he says, his objective in writing the play is to retrieve Ramanuja from the prison of the establishment. With this purpose in mind, he says that he has departed from the sources in certain significant ways. For instance, he would not give credence to the view that the Chola king was a religious fanatic as claimed by source narratives and biographies. Similarly, he argues that Ramanuja could not have gone all the way to Delhi to retrieve the image of Sampat Kumara. Therefore, rejecting the hagiographers' far-fetched claims, Indira Parthasarathy follows Alkondavilli Govindacharya's biography which offers a reasonable account of Ramanuja's adventurous journey to bring back the idol. Indira Parthasarathy is also disinclined to accept the explanation given for the three closed fingers of Alavandar at the time of his death. For him, the three unfulfilled wishes of Alavandar should have been high and sublime and not simplistic desires to perpetuate the names of Sage Vyasa and the Tamil mystic hymnist Nammazhwar. It is here that Indira Parthasarathy, by a typical gesture of rereading the original, brings in the caste question and makes it one of the prime concerns of Alavandar which he bequeaths to Ramanuja, namely the establishment of a casteless society. Indira Parthasarathy holds that the Vaishnava religion as practised and propagated by Ramanuja is nothing if not humanistic. Indira Parthasarathy has always been critical of blind, orthodox Brahminism. This play, unlike *Nandan Kathai*, offers a more positive space for affirming his ideology. In *Nandan Kathai,* the protagonist is not a Brahmin but a pariah. In *Ramanujar*, the protagonist is not only a Brahmin but also a Brahmin acharya/preceptor who embraces the pariah. It is no wonder then that the playwright holds the personality of Ramanuja dear to his heart. He is keen to demonstrate that Ramanuja was socially 'engaged' and that his metaphysics cannot be divorced from his sociology. Indira Parthasarathy goes to great lengths to project Ramanuja as a supreme idealist who embraces all of humanity. As an intellectual, the author refuses to legitimize caste by an appeal to the karma theory. Fortunately for him, there are innumerable instances in Ramanuja's life where the pontiff is compelled to do some rethinking when confronted with a challenging or even embarrassing social situation. The idealist image of Ramanuja that one finds in the play is also in conformity with the lofty personality that is projected in innumerable narratives.

However, one cannot help asking oneself whether this play has added one more work to the existing corpus of hagiographies on Ramanuja. Given Indira Parthasarathy's intellectual, interrogating, and sceptical temper, one would have been happier to see a more nuanced presentation of Ramanuja, especially in dealing with social pressures and situations. For example, in the originals, it is Maha Purna, one of Ramanuja's own teachers, who proves to be absolutely radical in nursing the ailing outcaste Maraner Nambi and daring to give him a Brahminical funeral when he dies. This, as noted earlier, causes an altercation between Maha Purna and Ramanuja where Ramanuja expresses some fear about completely doing away with the governing rules of the existing social order. What Indira Parthasarathy does in his play is to put whatever Maha Purna says into the mouth of Ramanuja, thereby taking away all the pressure one would face while dealing with a tense social situation. Had he followed the original, it would have given the reader of our times a better idea of how Ramanuja learnt gradually to question the social structure. Even in the hagiographies, such nuances are not ignored. In his eagerness if not anxiety to make Ramanuja a perfect human being, Indira Parthasarathy has allowed a simple dramatic contrast to operate between the orthodox Brahminical community connected to the temple and Ramanuja, the reformer. Carman, for example, points out that the Srirangam temple record *Koil Ozhugu* makes it clear that Ramanuja proceeded little by little to a thoroughgoing reorganization of temple administration. But his measures injured the interests of some quarters because they meant displacement of several temple functionaries, curtailment of the powers of others, and the provision of positions for a number of Ramanuja's own disciples (some of them his relatives, for example his nephew Dasarathi was made secretary) coming from a different group of Brahmins living in the region around Kanchi. The reasons why the old guard resented Ramanuja's actions are complicated. They include the animosity and reservations the southern group felt for the northern Kanchi group (Carman 1974: 34). Carman also raises the question of who succeeded Ramanuja to the pontificate at Srirangam. There are differing views on this, but Dasarathi's name does not figure in any of them. When asked about the switch of role between Maha Purna and Ramanuja, the playwright explained to me that he was writing a play not about Maha Purna but about Ramanuja. Even so, a closer adherence to the original would have given the modern reader a better understanding of the historical circumstances under which both Maha Purna and Ramanuja lived, surrounded by simmering hostility, and also of the strategies Ramanuja adopted to negotiate opposing forces. This would have given a true dramatic pressure to the situation in the play. However, Indira Parthasarathy has fully transformed the character Attuzhay from a meek girl into a bold radical confronting the mean-minded and scheming temple community. Many of the sources do not give such an impression of the girl, though Vaali's recent verse biography does highlight the ordeals faced by Maha Purna and his daughter because of their caring for a Panchama or person of the fifth caste.

Another feature of the play is the use of Greek theatrical convention, the *deus ex machina* (literally, 'the God descending on machine'). It is natural that in legends and hagiographies, divine intervention should come to the rescue of the protagonists in moments of crisis. Indira Parthasarathy, as a modern writer, has simply repeated the feature without problematizing it. This comes as a surprise because Parthasarathy has generally attempted to divest religion of its supernatural frills; in fact, in *Nandan Kathai*, he even ventured to denounce the supernatural dimension of religion as charlatanism disguised as transcendental revelation to promote the interests of the dominant community. In *Ramanujar*, perhaps he could not engage his intellectual energy towards demythicizing the claims of sanctity mainly because that would amount to divesting Ramanuja himself of his greatness and, consequently, shaking the very basis of Vaishnavism. In the hagiographies, there is a blatant use of miracles in narrating instances of resistance to Ramanuja's authority. For example, when Ramanuja undertook the customary spiritual tour after assuming charge of the Srirangam mutt, he attempted to introduce the pancharatra[9] mode of temple worship in the Anantapadmanabha Swamy temple in Thiruvananthapuram in Kerala. But the traditionally powerful Namboodiri priests apparently physically threw him out. The hagiography presents his removal in a metaphoric manner—he found himself on a cot in a temple town in Tamil Nadu when he woke up. This is attributed to divine intervention. Similarly, at the Puri Jagannath temple on the east coast in Orissa state, Ramanuja attempted the same but was spurned by the traditional priests, the pandas, and the locals, which reminds us of the fact that the temple was originally under the care of the tribals. Ramanuja is said to have been transported to Srikoormam in Andhra in a dream.

This is all evidence of how hagiography negotiates the resistance of 'little *récit*' to 'grand *récit*' through the sublimatory device of miracles.

Indira Parthasarathy has, however, employed the device of the *deus ex machina* critically in the scene where Attuzhay exhorts Ramanuja to expose the true colours of the Brahmin community in the temple opposing her father. Here the author typically projects the common man's voice as the voice of the Lord. In the Melukote episode too or the Karnataka sequence in general, it is difficult to avoid supernatural elements such as dreams, astral voices, revelations. For example, there is the ticklish question of Ramanuja going to Melukote in search of tiruman (fine white clay) which a devout Vaishnavite uses to make the mark of his faith on the designated parts of his body. The hagiographies give an account of Ramanuja getting a signal from Lord Tirunarayana to go to Yadavagiri to secure the white clay. The discovery is usually depicted in ecstatic terms. The epigraphist's line of enquiry is however typically different from the hagiographer's, as we have seen earlier. B.R. Gopal, the epigraphist, wonders whether the lure of the fine white clay was the real reason for Ramanuja's going to Melukote from Tondanur. He is of the opinion that the king took to the personality of Ramanuja and made endowments for the upkeep of the Tirunarayana temple. It is this cordial and respectful reception and patronage that Ramanuja received from the Hoysala king that must have prompted Ramanuja to move his headquarters in exile from Tondanur to Melukote. However, Alkondavilli Govindacharya cites the thirteenth-century diarist Buchanan who records that the white clay in Yadavagiri is indeed the finest; it was the decayed schistose mica which when boiled allowed a gleaming white mica to surface, which was used for making tiruman and this material was exported to other Vaishnava centres in the country (Govindacharya 1906 [2004: 162–3]).[10] Behind the supernatural, there is a material reality which must have prompted Ramanuja to seek residence in Melukote. Of course, as a playwright, Indira Parthasarathy cannot be expected to put such innumerable details into his work.

The rational approach of Indira Parthasarathy as a writer is evident in his handling of certain crucial events in Ramanuja's life. He refuses to indict the Chola king as sectarian hagiographers did for persecuting Ramanuja. In fact, nowhere in the play do we find the Chola king condemning Ramanuja and his sect. Indira Parthasarathy uses this chunk of Ramanuja's life story very objectively to demonstrate that religion appropriates political power. He does present in the court scenes the war of the righteous Vaishnavas against pettyfogging schemers in the garb of religion. In fact, he makes the king a sort of Pontius Pilate who did not know where the truth lay.

Hence, while we accept the historian M.S. Govindasamy's argument that the intra-Vaishnava feud was largely responsible for Ramanuja's predicament, one cannot completely discount the political dimension of this episode.

Indira Parthasarathy has a deconstructive turn of mind and a sceptical disposition as a social critic and writer. Deconstruction looks not so much for 'difference without' (as Barbara Johnson has pointed out) as for 'difference within'. If we stop at constructing binaries such as man/woman, God/man, Brahmin/pariah, we do not really read into the processes by which such structures are erected, be they social, material, metaphysical, or religious. When we read the various biographies of Ramanuja, we realize that he was not rejecting Hinduism or what is called 'Sanatana Dharma', but was trying to expose the weaknesses in the arguments of some of its proponents and adherents. That is certainly an instance of 'working the difference within'. However, not satisfied with such subversions, he, as an acharya or preceptor, went on to construct a religio-social discourse to accommodate the 'difference within'. Cyril Veliath, who has studied the mysticism of Ramanuja, points out that Ramanuja was within the Vaidiki fold in matters of initiation and ritual training, but recognized that spirit was above varna in matters of bhakti and prapatti. Apart from the enquiry into the philosophical premises of Ramanuja and their differences from those of *Advaita* which have been discussed by scholars of different persuasions, we have the interesting aspect that Ramanuja has himself become a trope, fascinating to biographers, poets, critics, and artists. The texts about him have become intertexts to other texts generating more texts. As mentioned earlier Indira Parthasarathy has a general deconstructive turn of mind. The deconstructive project initiates two processes: 1) to repeat an existing structure and 2) to undermine it. Perhaps here one may get an explanation to the puzzle that troubles the reader of this play on Ramanuja. Why should Indira Parthasarathy repeat the mode of hagiography if he wanted to highlight a differentiated trope of

Ramanuja? The answer lies in the dramatist's intention to undermine the significance or *tatparyam* of many such narratives, that is most narratives claimed that Ramanuja was favourably disposed to the lower castes, but in effect such a disposition did not operate unequivocally. In Indira Parthasarathy's play, Ramanuja aims at establishing a casteless society by questioning the existing philosophy of representation and construction. He constructs an anti-system of differentials opposed to the system of identity. Every deconstruction is itself a text with an aporia, with some inconsistency in need of deconstruction. Texts are about other texts. There is nothing outside of the text. Deconstruction brings in the notion of 'différance' which begets substitution and displacement, effective rupture and dissemination of sense. Thus in every text, we do not look for meaning as much as for its process. In this sense, the play *Ramanujar* is a text about other texts on Ramanuja using the episteme of Hindu society as its discourse centre. This subject has always fascinated Indira Parthasarathy, and he mercilessly treated it in his play *Nandan Kathai*. In the play *Ramanujar*, however, Indira Parthasarathy seems to go beyond deconstruction and look for a humanism which survives cynicism.

Notes

1. See 'Commentary on the Play' for gloss and explanation.
2. As J.B. Carman noted, relatively little detailed study of Ramanuja and the Sri Vaishnava tradition was conducted by western scholars. Earlier periods of Indian literary and cultural history were the point of interest of western orientalists and hence western students devoted more time to Sankara and the Advaita school (Carman 1974: 2).
3. The term 'Visishtadvaita', however, was not used by Ramanuja. It was used for the first time by a later-day Vaishnava scholar Sudarsanasuri in his commentary on Ramanuja's *Sri Bhashya* and *Vedantasara* (Veliath 1993: 34). It was only in the second half of the sixteenth century that the school of Ramanuja received that name.
4. F. Hardy in *Tamil Veda* (pp. 29–30, 70–1) is cited by Cyril Veliath to show the intricate difference between Ramanuja's position and that of Sankara. Ramanuja nowhere mentions the idea that the Sudra cannot undergo the initiation of the sacred thread or *upanayana* ceremony. Both Sankara and Ramanuja disqualified the Sudra from the performance of Vedic rites, but differed on the issue of *Brahmavidya* or ultimate knowledge. While Sankara defined it exclusively in

terms of what is expounded in the Upanishads, Ramanuja emphasized the experiential knowledge of Brahman (Veliath 1993: 124, n. 53).

5. Popular utterances and actions attributed to Ramanuja claim that, according to him, even a person who does not stand within the Ashrama, is qualified to receive knowledge. However, Cyril Veliath cites Hardy's observation that although hagiographers highlight Ramanuja's more liberal attitude towards the Sudras as compared to Sankara's, Ramanuja's commentary in *Badarayana Sutra* states that Sudras are not qualified to receive the knowledge of Brahman (Veliath 1993: 4).

6. "பெரியநம்பி மாறனேறி நம்பியை ப்ரஹ்மமேதத்தாலே ஸம்ஸ்கரித்துப் பள்ளிப்படுத்தருள, இதுகேட்டு எம்பெருமானார் நம்பி ஸ்ரீபாத்தேறச் சென்று தண்டன் ஸமர்ப்பித்து, "சீயா! ஸம்ஸாரம் சிலுகிடாதபடி அடியேன் ஒருவழியாலே வேலியிட்டு வர, தேவரீர் ஒருவழியாலே பிரித்தருளர நின்றதே! என்று விண்ணப்பஞ் செய்ய ...." (GPP 6000: 237).

7. See 'Commentary on the Play'.

8. Kuresa tricked their ancestor out of his inherited status as the high priest. However, the priest was given the name Amudhanar (which means sweet-tongued) by Ramanuja and was given a new function—to chant the 4000. Carman remarks on the panegyric he wrote on Ramanuja praising him. 'It is remarkable that Ramanuja should have been so highly praised by the man whose authority in the temple he had so seriously diminished' (Carman 1974: 38).

9. Pancharatra is 'a designation of the ancient vaisnavite system,' according to F. Otto Schrader (1916 [1995: 28]), referring to 'the five-fold self-manifestation of God' (ibid.: 29). Schrader explains, 'The Pancarâtra teaches a chain ... of emanations each emanation, except the first, originating from an anterior emanation; and thus the favourite image of the process has ... become that of one flame proceeding from another flame' (ibid.: 40). Vaishnava scholars also hold that the term suggests that Lord Vishnu Himself gave instructions to five sages to remove the ignorance of devotees.

10. Govindacharya refers to some notes from the famous Rice's *Epigraphica Carnatica* Vol. III. 20, particularly to Inscription 80. Sr. which grants the title to the sacred white clay at Melukote, said to have been discovered by Ramanujacharya (AKVG 1906 [2004: 162]).

AUTHOR'S PREFACE

Ramanujar, who was born in AD 1017, is said to have lived for a hundred and twenty years.

The ancient books which chronicle the life of Ramanujar— *Guruparamparai Prabhavam, Yadiraja Vaibhavam, Ramanuja Champu, Ramanuja Divya Charitam, Divyasuri Charitam, Koilozhugu Yadiraja Saptadi, Yadiraja Vamsati*—view him with devotional fervour. So it is not surprising that the story of his life and the history of his times have been the subject of imaginative extensions and constructions.

Indian consciousness does not see time as a linear arithmetic progression of sequential events. Therefore, the historical explanation of events in terms of chronology and causality is not something that we should expect to find in the history of our ancestors. It is thus impossible, when we dramatize the life of someone who lived for a hundred and twenty years, to see that history in the light of the logic of events.

It is said that a straight line represents the shortest distance between two points. But a 'straight line' is itself a convenient fiction. The sequence of events dramatized in this play as scenes is a piece of imaginative construction too that we undertake in order to fully understand one of the great men of Indian history.

The aim of this play is to see how someone who lived nine hundred years ago is very much our contemporary.

Ramanujar was not the founder of the Vaishnavite religion. Well before his time, men like Nathamuni, Uyyakondan, Manakkal Nambi, and Alavandar, drawn by the devotional acts of the Azhwars, had laid the base for Vaishnavite doctrines. Ramanujar gave shape to those doctrines and also paved the way for the common people to have access to those ideas which had been regarded as sacrosanct and exclusivist.

The Advaita philosophy, as expounded by Sankara during the period of Buddhist dominance, was a historical necessity. But the people who misunderstood his philosophy of *maya*, harped on the transience of human life and, in fact, took the stand that the world itself was an object to be hated.

Ramanujar lived after Sankara. He realized that while the concept of *nirgunabrahmam* ('attributeless godhead') was useful for attaining intellectual clarity, it could not be a spontaneously felt experience for the common masses who constituted the majority in society. Therefore, he erected, as the pillars of the edifice that he himself built, the path of devotion (bhakti), which was the fit path for all people, and its ultimate end, *prapatti* (the philosophy of *saranagati* or surrender). It should not be forgotten that even Sankara, at a later stage, had felt the need to sing the *Bhajagovindam* song, emphasizing bhakti.

From a psychological viewpoint, the individual cannot exist without God. That is why, till today, no philosophy which does not acknowledge the existence of God has succeeded. Events which happen have to have meaning. That is why Einstein, the greatest scientist of this century, said, 'God does not play dice'. If we image God as the ultimate meaning of events, then the journey of life becomes interesting. Ramanujar said that when we realize this point fully, *chit* ('atman') and *achit* ('body') are both one with God; and when we feel such a state experientially, life becomes an enjoyable journey. Ramanujar imaged God as *Bhuvanasundaran* ('one who embodies the beauty of the world') because he regarded bhakti itself as a *rasa*. The *aham* songs of the Azhwars, conceived in the *nayaka-nayaki bhava* also reinforce the idea of bhakti as a rasa.

Caste discrimination is the bane of Vedic religion. Even more outrageous was the justification of high and low births as the fruit of karma. Ramanujar rejected caste discrimination absolutely and fully. His first Vaishnavite guru was Tirukkacchi Nambi who belonged to the Vaisya community. Ramanujar must have posed this question: maintaining that chit and achit are both inseparable attributes of godhead, how can we accept that there are differences of high and low so far as achit is concerned? If we do accept such differences, then we must ascribe those deficiencies to God too. But then God is Brahman; the word is also derivable from Brihat. And Brahman means 'a unique thing complete in itself and possessing all the perfect attributes'.

In order to do away with caste discrimination, Ramanujar declared that Vaishnavism belonged to everyone. He made the *Panchamas* (the people of the fifth caste who had been relegated to the fringes of society) Vaishnavites and called them Tirukkulattar (people of the holy community). The historian Buchanan[1] has described, with authentic evidence, the service that the Tirukkulattar rendered, standing shoulder to shoulder with Ramanujar, in building the Vishnu temple at Melukote and in retrieving the *utsava* deity whom Ramanujar called *Chellapillai* ('darling child'). Buchanan further tells us that Ramanujar issued orders for conferring special honours on the Tirukkulattar in the temples of the Karnataka state at Melukote, Srirangapatnam, and Belur. Rice's *Gazetteer* of AD 1897 describes in detail this practice which has been handed down from generation to generation.

Another interesting fact of Ramanujar's life is his visit to Delhi and his retrieval, from the Turkish sultan, of Sampat Kumaran, the utsava deity of the Melukote temple. Even now there exists a shrine called *Turuka Nachiyar* in each of the major Vishnu temples. Even in the present times, at the Srirangam temple, on the day of the observance of *Pahal Pattu* during the *Ekadasi* festival, there is the practice of dressing Lord Vishnu in a *lungi* in the fashion of Muslims and granting *darshan* to the Turukka (Turkish) Nachiyar.

Atkondavilli Govindachariyar, who has chronicled the life of Ramanujar, has treated this story quite artistically. In the traditional accounts, this Turkish king is referred to as 'Emmadu Rayan'. Govindachariyar maintains that 'Emmadu' might be a variant of 'Mohammad' and 'Rayan' means 'king'. The Turkish king need not have reigned in Delhi. Even in those times there were minor Muslim rulers in regions north of the Hoysala country. Therefore 'Emmadu Rayan' could well have been a minor Muslim ruler of a neighbouring state.

Prabhakar's *Yavanapriya* tells of the marriage of the 'Turkish princess' to 'Sampat Kumaran'. During a Hindu marriage ceremony, the *gotra*s (lineages) of the bride and the bridegroom are usually announced. *Yavanapriya* says that the gotras in this case were the *Harita* gotra for Sampat Kumaran (Chellapillai), because he was Ramanujar's 'son' and *Gargiya* gotra for the Sultani (the Turkish princess). According to Govindachariyar, all foreigners were in the classical Sanskrit tradition called Yavanas, and so 'Sultani' becomes 'Yavani'. Since all Greeks (Yavanas) were assigned the Gargiya gotram, it must have been given to the 'Sultani' as well. Though this sounds fanciful, there does seem to be an element of historical truth in it.

I am quite aware that it is no easy task to dramatize the life of Ramanujar which is so full of historical as well as highly imaginative events. What impelled me to write a play on Ramanujar was the fact that he was not only a thinker but a great man of action.

During the days when Sanskrit, like English today, had currency only among intellectuals and was the sole language of worship, it was Ramanujar who changed the trend and installed Tamil in the inner shrine of temples so that God could be worshipped easily by the poor masses who constituted the majority. It was this accessibility that made it possible for everyone to accept the Vaishnavite religion without the discrimination of caste.

Ramanujar again was the first Vedic religious leader to accord women a status equal to that of men and to accept them as disciples. In Vaishnavite discourse, Narayana is called Tirumagal Kelvan, after the interpretive tradition created by Ramanujar. The major women who were part of his mutt were Andal (the wife of Kuresar), Ponnachi, Kongu Piratti, Tiruven Paricharattu Ammai, Tiruvettaru Ammai, Tiruvananthapurathu Ammai, and others.

It must be mentioned here that this play departs from the *Guruparampara* accounts in some places. While talking about the three unfulfilled wishes of Alavandar, these accounts say that the first two of these wishes were naming Vaishnavite children after Veda Vyasa and his father Parasara. Alavandar is said, in these accounts, to have mentioned these before he attained Tirunadu. When, however, we consider that his third unfulfilled wish was the writing of a *vyakhyanam* (commentary) on the *Vyasasutra*s, we wonder whether he would have regarded his failure to bestow those names on Vaishnavite children as such a serious omission. That is why I have changed the first two 'wishes', to bring them on a par with the third. When we remember that Maraner Nambi, who belonged to the fifth caste, was a disciple of Alavandar, it seems certain that it was Alavandar who shaped Ramanuja's thought.

In the narratives of the Vaishnavite tradition, again, the Chola king has been the object of denunciation and has been portrayed as a religious fanatic. It is not clear, however, which Chola king this was. Ramanujar, who lived around a hundred and twenty years, must have seen the reign of five Chola kings. When we look at historical documents, we can guess that it was perhaps Kulothunga I. But when we consider that he also bore the title of 'Sapta Vishnu Vardhanan', the question arises as to whether he could have been a Saivite fanatic.

Those were the times when religion and politics were closely related all over the world. Royal power was dependent on the support of religious leaders. Ramanujar's tenets ran contrary to those of other religious leaders who enjoyed popularity. The fear that Ramanujar's religion might destroy ritualistic practices as well as the very structure of the caste system must have existed among both the Vaishnavites and the Saivites. It is also a fact of history that no king could reign while antagonizing religious majorities.

It is for these reasons that, in this play, the Chola king has been portrayed as initiating action against Ramanujar in the most reluctant fashion. The history of Christianity tells us that the Roman governor (Pilate) washed his hands after delivering judgment against Jesus Christ. The Ramanujar affair must have constituted a crisis for the Chola king. The Vaishnavites as well as the Saivites were opposed to Ramanujar. We should understand the dilemma the king must have found himself in. That is why he has not been depicted in this play as a hardened religious fanatic.

As Ramanujar is believed to have lived for a hundred and twenty years, certain problems may arise when the play is staged. He appears in the first scene as a youth and it is necessary to show him as progressively older in the subsequent scenes. He was 25 at the beginning of the play, 32 at the time of his renunciation, 79 when he went to Melukote, and 83 when he raised the Tirunarayanan temple at Melukote. He stayed at Melukote till the age of 99. He returned to Srirangam when he was 101 and he attained Tirunadu at the age of 120. The chronicles say that he remained healthy and strong till the very end and so there is nothing wrong in portraying him in the same state from the age of 60 till the end.

The play ends with Ramanujar declaring Kuresar's son as his (Ramanujar's) heir.

No sets are needed for the performance of this play. The events take place in Kanchi, Srirangm, the Nilgiri forests, Melukote, and the country ruled by the Muslim king. Indications of these places are provided in the text itself. However, it is not strictly necessary to follow these indications either. It is a matter of how the director's imagination shapes the places and events. I would like to say, however, that elaborate stage settings might interfere with the play of ideas in the drama.

The aim of the play is to make readers and audience see Ramanujar as our contemporary. A non-conformist thinker of a certain time is always shut up in a prison of the establishment by his own followers in subsequent times. It is my contention that we should rescue Ramanujar, a revolutionary in his own times, from such a prison and understand him fully. It is wrong, at the same time, to evaluate him by the yardstick of modern values. One truth, however, we can assert with certainty. From ancient times till now, the only yardstick that can establish the prime movers of history is their humanitarianism. There is no religion greater than humanitarianism.

Notes

1.   A thirteenth-century diarist also cited by the biographer Alkondavilli Govindacharya (1906 [2004]).

PROLOGUE

(*As the curtain goes up, the stage is dark. Thunder, lightning, and then the noise of heavy rain. The light focuses on the portion of the stage where one person can lie down. A man now enters, thoroughly drenched in the rain and seeking shelter. He approaches the lighted portion. It is the passage immediately beyond the threshold of a house. Shivering in the cold, he lies down there.*

After a while, another man, also seeking shelter from the rain, walks to the lighted portion. The one who was lying down gets up and makes room for him. Both of them sit. After some time, a third man enters, also trying to find shelter. The two who were sitting make room for him.

All three now stand. They notice a fourth coming near them. That fourth person is not visible to the audience.

In an instant, the whole stage is steeped in a flood of light.

Then all the three prostrate themselves in the direction from which the light emanates ...)

THE FIRST (*rising, sings*):

Pasuram[1]

The earth is my lamp, the vast sea is the oil, and the radiant sun the flame. I offer this garland of songs at the feet of the effulgent discus-bearing Lord, that we may cross the ocean of misery.'[2]

THE SECOND: Love is my lamp, ardour the oil, and my devout thoughts the wick. With my heart melting, here I light this lamp of supreme knowledge and offer this Tamil garland of wisdom to Narayana.[3]

THE THIRD: Lo, here I behold, this day, Goddess Lakshmi on the ocean-hued golden frame of my Lord. I behold in His hands the fiery golden discus and the dextral conch.[4]

(*When they finish singing, all three stand entranced ... A voice is heard.*)

THE VOICE: Poykai, Bhootama, and Pey are the first three Azhwars. It is they who taught the world the humanitarian truth that if there is space for one person to lie down, two can sit in it and three can stand. They saw God as the fourth there. This is the beginning of the story of Vaishnavism. After the Azhwars came the acharyas. The first among them was Nathamuni. After him, Uyyakondar. Then Manakkal Nambi followed by Alavandar. After Alavandar, Ramanujar .... The play begins in the last days of Alavandar.[5]

(The light fades out.)

ACT I

SCENE 1

TIRUVARANGAM[6]

(*Darkness as the curtain goes up. After a few seconds, a stream of blue light focuses on Alavandar who is sitting on an altar. Dim light on the disciples who stand round him in two rows. Alavandar is an old man. His eyes closed, he is sitting in the* padmasana *posture.*

The song that was heard as background music when the curtain went up, is now heard loud and clear. Alavandar is evidently lost in the music.

It is morning.)

Pasuram

Behold, the lotus has bloomed in profusion, the sun has risen from the sea. Slender-waisted women with curly locks step out of the river onto the river-bank, squeezing their hair dry and putting on their clothes. O Lord Ranga, surrounded by the surging waters of the Kaveri, bless this lowly serf, Tondaradippodi, bearer of the flower basket, that he may serve your devotees. O Lord, arise![7]

(*When the music stops, the temple bell rings. The conch is sounded. Alavandar opens his eyes. There is rapture on his face. He looks at the disciples on both sides, then closes his eyes.*)

ALAVANDAR (*in a clear, soft tone*): The Lord calls.

(*Silence for a while.*)

ALAVANDAR: The end is the only certainty. That is life.

(*Silence for a while.*)

ALAVANDAR (*startled*): Sacrilege! The Vaishnavite never dies.

(*Silence again.*)

ALAVANDAR: How can there be an end to his life? He is a player in an endless game.

(*Silence for a few seconds.*)

ALAVANDAR (*opens his eyes*): My dreams were so many, deeds so few. (*Sighs.*)
ALAVANDAR: A casteless society. Salvation even for the lowliest. That was my first wish.

(*Counts on his fingers.*)

ALAVANDAR: The narrow, cribbed, and confined Vaishnava dharma should expand and enlarge beyond bounds. That was my next wish.

(*Counts on his fingers again.*)

ALAVANDAR: Planted with a wet paddy seed in the field of the heart— that is our religion—Vaishnavism. It is the outlook of the heart. It is with that outlook that I wished to write a commentary on the *Brahmasutra*. I couldn't. That was my third wish.

(*He folds the third finger. The fingers stay folded. Silence for a few seconds.*)

ALAVANDAR: My first mission is done. Slum-dweller Tambi Maraner Nambi is my disciple ... the first task is done. To continue the mission—he will come.

(*The disciples look at one another. They don't understand who Alavandar refers to when he says 'he'.*)

ALAVANDAR: The other day I saw him. At Kanchi. *Perarulalan*[8] said, 'Alavandar, this is your heir!' What presence! What radiance! Rama's younger sibling—Ramanujan!

(*The disciples look at one another again.*)

ALAVANDAR: I have sent Periya Nambi to fetch him. Continuity is the principle of life.

(*The temple bell rings. There is joy on Alavandar's face. ... He closes his eyes.*)

ALAVANDAR (*in a very soft voice*): Sing *Soozh visumbu*.

(*The disciples sing.*)

Pasuram

Clouds in the sky blew horns like heralds, waves in the ocean clapped
and danced. The seven continents stood with offerings in their hands,
filled with joy at the sight of the eternally celebrated Lord Narayana.[9]

(*There is peace on Alavandar's face. He sits motionless. The three fingers
remain folded. The temple bell keeps ringing. Darkness.*

*When the lights come on after a few seconds, enter, from the left side of the
forestage, Ramanujar and Periya Nambi. Ramanujar follows Periya Nambi.
Periya Nambi is past middle age. A countenance full of peace.*

*Ramanujar is a young man, tall, well-built, with a commanding
presence. There is an expression of lucidity and firmness on his face.*

*Both of them start a little when they see Alavandar in the padmasana
posture. Ramanujar moves quickly towards Alavandar and looks intently
at his countenance then at the countenance of Periya Nambi, who has moved
close to him, then at the disciples who are immersed in grief. Periya Nambi is
unable to control his sobs. Ramanujar holds his hands.*)

RAMANUJAR: You are my guru. Please forgive my impertinence. Is there
any death, beginning, or end for a Vaishnavite?

(*Alavandar's disciples look at Ramanujar with wonder. The very words
of Alavandar! They guess that this must be Ramanujar ...*)

DISCIPLE 1: You are ...
RAMANUJAR: Ramanujan.[10]
DISCIPLE 2: We guessed that when you came with Periya Nambi.
DISCIPLE 3: Those were the very words that Alavandar spoke ...
DISCIPLE 4: Before he reached Tirunadu.[11]
DISCIPLE 1: The Vaishnavite never dies. ... Is there any beginning or
end to his life?
DISCIPLE 2: Alavandar had identified you ...
DISCIPLE 3: You are his heir.
DISCIPLE 4: This is the message he has left ...

(*As they prostrate themselves before him, he tries to stop them. Not
comprehending, he looks at Periya Nambi. Periya Nambi stands gazing at
Alavandar's body. He observes the three fingers folded on Alavandar's right
hand. He is puzzled by this. He looks at the disciples, as if to ask why it is
like that.*)

DISCIPLE 1: Alavandar had three unfulfilled wishes.

DISCIPLE 2: A casteless society. Salvation even for the lowliest.

DISCIPLE 3: The Vaishnava dharma which now lies confined within narrow limits should expand beyond bounds.

DISCIPLE 4: A commentary on the *Brahmasutra*.

DISCIPLES 1, 2, 3, and 4: Thus the three folded fingers represent unfulfilled wishes ...

(*Ramanujar stands for a while looking at those fingers. There is resolve on his face ...*)

RAMANUJAR: If we have *bhakti*, that is the greatest strength. If we have divine grace, everything we see is *Vaikuntam*.[12] God represents the bounds of the realm of possibility. It is towards those bounds that my journey hereafter will be directed. It is my duty to carry out Alavandar's wishes. They will be fulfilled. And that is certain.

(*The disciples together chant, Om Namo Narayanaya. Ramanujar prostrates himself before Alavandar's corporal body. The temple bell rings. The light focuses on Alavandar's body and then fades.*)

SCENE 2

KANCHI

(*As the lights come on, enter Ramanujar from the forestage R. Tirukkachi Nambi enters from L. He is middle aged, with a dark complexion. The music which is heard now continues to be heard in the background for a few minutes. Ramanujar moves to prostrate himself before Tirukkachi Nambi who stops him.*)

Pasuram

The Lord who resides in the well-fortified city of Kanchi, worshipped by all the worlds in Patakam, the Lord who rained arrows on the mighty chest of the Lanka king Ravana and bestowed his kingdom on his younger brother Vibhishana—may we chant His name, it is indeed Namo Narayana.[13]

(*It is morning.*)

TIRUKKACHI NAMBI (*in a startled tone*): The obeisance of the Brahmin—
is that for *me*?

RAMANUJAR: Does it behove Alavandar's disciple to talk thus? There is
no Brahmin or Vaisya for the Vaishnavite ...

TIRUKKACHI NAMBI: How then does one live out the fruits of karma?

RAMANUJAR: If we cultivate the paddy of bhakti, won't the weed of
karma die out?

(*Tirukkachi Nambi remains silent, and then smiles, as if to point out
that what Ramanujar said had not happened so far.*)

RAMANUJAR (*smiling*): Why this hesitation in accepting what I said? Has
the experience of Kanchi Purna[14] been different?

TIRUKKACHI NAMBI (*smiling*): Kkachi Nambi knows just this—caste has
not disappeared even with the efforts of Alavandar. The son of a
Chetty must stand at a distance from the Brahmin, mustn't he?

RAMANUJAR (*with feeling*): There is some good in the leadership of
Vaishnavism passing to me. The arrogance of caste shall no more
exist among Vaishnavites.

(*Tirukkachi Nambi grips Ramanujar's shoulders with joy and pride.
Ramanujar bows his head towards him.*)

RAMANUJAR: *Ayya*, I have a wish. *Gurunathar*[15] should not deny it.

TIRUKKACHI NAMBI: What?

RAMANUJAR: Tomorrow morning, you must have *amudhu*[16] at my
house.

(*Tirukkachi Nambi looks a little surprised at this.*)

TIRUKKACHI NAMBI: What is the occasion?

RAMANUJAR (*smiles*): That you are coming to have food with us is the occasion.

TIRUKKACHI NAMBI (*hesitating*): She ... your wife ...

RAMANUJAR: My path is her path too.

(*Tirukkachi Nambi stands silent for a few seconds, then smiles.*)

RAMANUJAR: If you can't come tomorrow ... (*reflecting*)

TIRUKKACHI NAMBI: I will come tomorrow ...

(*They bow to each other and take leave. Darkness. When the lights come
on, Ramanujar's wife, Tanjamma, is cutting vegetables sitting in the middle*)

of the rear stage. Though she is a beautiful woman, her beauty is hidden by the permanent scowl on her face. She looks like one who never learnt how to smile.

Ramanujar enters the forestage from L. There is joy on his face. And an eagerness to share the joy with his wife.)

RAMANUJAR: Tanjamma ... Tanjamma ...

(She looks up at him. She doesn't seem eager to share his happiness. Ramanujar picks up the mat kept in the corner, unrolls and spreads it before her, and sits. Tanjamma continues to cut vegetables.)

RAMANUJAR: Tirukkachi Nambi comes to our house tomorrow to have food.

(Tanjamma, startled, looks up at him.)

RAMANUJAR: Why, isn't that good news?

(Tanjamma doesn't reply but continues to cut vegetables.)

RAMANUJAR: Why this silence?
TANJAMMA *(looking down)*: Tomorrow is a *Purattasi* Saturday.[17]
RAMANUJAR: Yes, I know. We are truly blessed that Kanchi Purna comes to visit us tomorrow.

(Tanjamma looks up at him quickly but bends her head immediately to resume cutting vegetables. Her indifference annoys him.)

RAMANUJAR: I don't understand your silence.
TANJAMMA *(sarcastic)*: Nice guest to have on an auspicious day!
RAMANUJAR *(pretending not to have caught her sarcasm)*: Nice words!
TANJAMMA *(angry)*: You belong to a Somayaji family, let not the thought slip your mind.
RAMANUJAR: Kanchi Purna is my guru. Isn't a guru the same as one's father?

(Tanjamma attempts a smile. The smile doesn't look natural on her hard countenance.)

RAMANUJAR *(smiling)*: You had forgotten how to smile, and now you do. Isn't that a good outcome of the coming visit?
TANJAMMA *(angrily)*: The son of a Chetty is my father-in-law. That is a nice outcome?

(*Anger shows on Ramanujar's face, but he contains it. He rises and paces for a while. He had not expected that Tanjamma would take the news in this way. There is now more pain than anger on his face.*)

RAMANUJAR (*suddenly, turning towards Tanjamma and in a firm voice*): There will be a feast for him tomorrow at our house. The Vaishnavite does not go back on his word.

(*He exits from the forestage L, with a pained look. Tanjamma stands like a statue. Darkness.*)

SCENE 3

(*After a few seconds, when the lights come on, Tirukkachi Nambi enters from L forestage. He stands for a while, rather uncertain, looking towards the pial[18] at the centre, and then walks towards the pial. It is morning.*)

TIRUKKACHI NAMBI: It is my humble self ...

(*He stops and stands a few steps before the entrance to the house, which is at the C of the rear stage. Silence for a while.*)

TIRUKKACHI NAMBI (*a little loudly*): It is my humble self ...

(*Tanjamma enters from the opening in the rear stage.*)

TANJAMMA (*in a voice showing no emotion*): He is not at home. You can eat and go.

(*Nambi is a little shocked at this.*)

NAMBI: I will come later.
TANJAMMA: It is his order and it is my duty to carry it out.

(*Nambi does not know what he should do. He wonders whether Ramanujar would have asked her to serve him even if he himself was not at home. He stands silent.*)

TANJAMMA: Please sit on the pial. I will serve you food.

(*This is another shock for Nambi. He is also worried that Ramanujar might feel unhappy if he went away without eating. He stands, confused.*)

TANJAMMA: Please sit.

(She goes in, without waiting for his reply. Darkness. When the lights come on, Tanjamma is seen washing the pial. As she is doing so, Ramanujar enters from L forestage. He goes towards the rear stage. She continues washing the pial pretending that she had not noticed his coming. Ramanujar is puzzled.)

RAMANUJAR: What are you doing? Why wash the pial at this time?
TANJAMMA *(without looking at him)*: Atithi puja[19] is over.
RAMANUJAR: I don't understand.
TANJAMMA: That Vaisya came. Hospitality was shown to him.
RAMANUJAR: Even before I returned? I went to his house, he wasn't there.
TANJAMMA: It seems he had some urgent work. I served him food. He has left.

(As if suddenly remembering, Ramanujar looks at the pial that she has just washed clean. There is anger on his face.)

RAMANUJAR: You served him food on the pial, isn't that so?

(She is silent.)

RAMANUJAR: The place has been defiled by the Vaisya's sitting there, so you are cleansing it, isn't that so?

(She is silent.)

RAMANUJAR: So you didn't tell him that I had actually gone to fetch him?

*(She is silent.
Extremely pained, he looks at her. She stands motionless, like a statue.)*

RAMANUJAR: Does orthodoxy consist in crushing the *aniccha* flower?

(Seeing that she has not answered any of his questions, he exits, disappointment reflected on his face.)

SCENE 4

(When the lights come on after a few seconds, Ramanujar is seated on the pial. He seems to be awaiting someone's arrival. A middle-aged person enters from L forestage. He looks destitute. He walks towards Ramanujar. Ramanujar gets off the pial with a smile. It is morning.)

RAMANUJAR: I have been waiting for you.

VISITOR: It got late. I am sorry.

RAMANUJAR: Why do you look so weary?

(*The visitor hesitates. He wipes the sweat with his upper cloth.*)

RAMANUJAR: Well, if you do not wish to tell me ...

VISITOR: I am h ... u ... n ... g ... r ... y.

RAMANUJAR: Were you hesitant to say just this? Eat when you are
hungry ... That is the food code. Work only after you eat. That is
the code of life. First food for you. (*He looks inside and calls.*)
Tanjamma ...

(*Tanjamma comes out after a few seconds. She looks at the visitor.*)

RAMANUJAR: He is hungry.

TANJAMMA: Isn't he going to give you a bath with oil?

RAMANUJAR: What he needs first is food for his stomach.

TANJAMMA: There is nothing to eat. I haven't started cooking yet.

(*Ramanujar does not believe her. He looks closely at her and then goes
in. Tanjamma follows him. The visitor stands for a few seconds and then
leaves. Ramanujar brings cooked rice in a vessel. He is struck with sorrow
when he sees that the visitor has left. Tanjamma comes out now.*)

RAMANUJAR (*angrily*): Aren't you happy now? The one who came
has left.

TANJAMMA: Who is to have food first, *Perumal*[20] or someone on the street?

RAMANUJAR: Food first for the hungry. That is God's wish. If you deny
food to a poor visitor, the Merciful One will not forgive you.

TANJAMMA: Is everything I do wrong?

RAMANUJAR: You said there was no food. That was a lie. He was a self-
respecting soul. He went away without accepting charity.

(*Tanjamma stands silent for a while, then goes in. Tired, Ramanujar
sits on the pial.*)

RAMANUJAR: Oh God, grant me patience ...

(*The lights fade.*)

SCENE 5

(When the lights come on after a few seconds, Periya Nambi and Ramanujar enter from L forestage. It is morning.)

PERIYA NAMBI: I came to Kanchi in order to take you to Tiruvarangam. The spell of Lord Varada's charm still keeps me bound here.

RAMANUJAR: It is my good fortune. How much I have learnt from you!

PERIYA NAMBI (*smiling*): Just as Krishna learnt from Sage Santipi![21]

RAMANUJAR: Pride is a poisonous tree. And praise is its seed. Are Krishna and I the same? I have not earned the rewards of penance, nor do I have the finer intelligence. It was you and Alavandar who made me, who was nought, into something of substance.

PERIYA NAMBI: You are the one who is going to ascend the throne of Alavandar. When shall we go to Tiruvarangam?

RAMANUJAR: When the Lord of Kanchi ordains it.

PERIYA NAMBI (*smiles*): Very soon shall we be blessed with His grace.

(He takes leave and goes. Darkness. When the lights come on we see at C Tanjamma and Periya Nambi's wife. Periya Nambi's wife is about 30. She is plainly dressed. She seems to know very clearly what her rights are. We should imagine there to be a well at the centre and Tanjamma to be 'drawing water' with 'a metal pot'. Nambi's wife is standing near her, waiting to 'draw water'. Tanjamma's 'pot' makes contact with Nambi's wife's pot. Tanjamma gives her a scorching look.)

TANJAMMA (*irritated*): Defiled.

NAMBI'S WIFE (*shocked*): Defiled?

TANJAMMA: Yes … it is defilement. The Asoori family is known for its *acharam*[22].

NAMBI'S WIFE: What are you saying?

TANJAMMA: The south is below the north. Tiruvarangam is below Kanchi. Don't you understand?

NAMBI'S WIFE: Please think before you speak.

TANJAMMA: I am not in the habit of thinking before speaking. I am a fool. Will that do for you?

NAMBI'S WIFE: Did I say you were a fool? It was your husband who put us up at your home. What a noble soul he is!

TANJAMMA: Lots of people have said that and spoilt him. We have had enough of that. The reputation of the Asoori family has been sullied because of him. Hereafter it is my responsibility to protect our caste.

(Nambi's wife looks at her closely for a while, and goes away. Tanjamma stands there frozen like a statue. Ramanujar, who has entered from forestage L during the altercation, observes them. There is distress on his face. After Nambi's wife leaves, he walks towards Tanjamma. She looks at him, surprised, wondering if he has heard their exchange. Ramanujar stops near her. He does not look at her. The way he stands and the way he looks reveal that he knows everything.)

TANJAMMA *(guardedly)*: She was the one ...

RAMANUJAR *(steadily)*: I have not asked you anything.

TANJAMMA: Is it wrong to be concerned about defilement?

RAMANUJAR: Nothing is wrong. It is only our conjugal life that is wrong.

TANJAMMA: What wrong did I do?

RAMANUJAR: What wrong didn't you do? You cast Kkachi Nambi aside, as though he were scum. Where was the defilement? In your mind or in his caste? You denied food to someone who came hungry ... was it *ahankaram* or *acharam* that made you do that? Today, you have insulted Periya Nambi's wife. What wrong haven't you done? *(Silence for a few seconds.)* No, the mistake is mine. ... There should be compatibility of hearts for conjugal union. If that is missing ...

(Silence for a while.)

RAMANUJAR *(suddenly, turning towards her)*: Why this facade of 'husband and wife'?

(Tanjamma looks at him, shocked. He paces for a while.)

RAMANUJAR: Our paths are different. They can never meet. It is wise for us to live apart. Here and now, I renounce the life of a married man. I shall hereafter live for society.

TANJAMMA *(shocked)*: What is this? I did wrong ...

(She makes to prostrate before him.)

RAMANUJAR *(stopping her and picking her up)*: No ... Let me go my way. All my things will be yours from now. There is nothing that I shall call my own hereafter. You go your way. I shall not interfere. That is best for both of us.

(*He walks away quickly through L forestage. Tanjamma stands frozen. The lights fade.*)

SCENE 6

(*When the lights come on after a few seconds, we see Ramanujar at C, kneeling, praying with palms opened upwards and raised towards the heavens. The lights focus on him. The rest of the stage is dark.*)

RAMANUJAR: Oh Merciful One! My goal is service to society. That is impossible within matrimony. The Vaishnavism of my vision will stride the whole world, even as you strode the universe as Trivikrama. Equal justice to all is the life-breath of my Vaishnavism. Grant me the courage of conviction and mental strength to establish such a Vaishnavism. I will find human bonds through *sanyasa*. That is certain.

(*He closes his eyes. Darkness.*)

SCENE 7

(*Dim lights on the stage. Two figures, male and female, walk slowly round the stage. It is night. The hoot of an owl and the howl of a fox indicate that they are passing through a forest region. The woman has a cloth bundle in her hands. We see that they are a married couple. When they have gone round the stage three times, another man enters from forestage L. He looks starved, a mere skeleton, and he walks with faltering steps. When he enters, the couple are in the R corner of the rear stage. He holds his left hand over his eyes and looks at them. They walk round the stage, approach him, and look up at him.*)

HE: Swami, I come from afar. I must get to Kooram. I seem to have lost my way. Please ...

THE HUSBAND: What are you going to Kooram for?

HE: They said Kuresar's house is open for guests day and night. My very ears are dulled with hunger.

(*The husband looks at the wife. She opens the cloth bundle in her hands, takes out a gold cup from it, and ties the bundle again and gives it to her husband. He has been talking to the other man and hasn't noticed her taking out the gold cup.*)

THE HUSBAND: You need not go in search of Kuresan. Kuresan has come looking for you.

(*Kuresar hands him the bundle he received from his wife. There is a smile on his face. The alms-seeker is shocked, confused whether he should accept the bundle which he has taken almost involuntarily.*)

THE ALMS-SEEKER: I don't understand. Are y ... o ... u Kuresar? And why ... on this forest path?

KURESAR (*smiling*): This is not a forest path ... It is the path to *swarga*, the merciful path that will take us to Ramanujar. It is the path of dharma, which has given us this privilege of giving you food, even at this stage, when we have renounced everything.

THE ALMS-SEEKER: Kuresar, what is this, you have given me your food bundle? Forgive me. I don't ...

(*He tries to hand the bundle back to Kuresar, but the latter refuses to take the bundle from him.*)

THE ALMS-SEEKER: Must I have food when you are starving?

KURESAR: Your body has been ravaged by hunger. All that we see is a skeleton. It is you alone who needs this food. Please take it and satisfy your hunger. We will take leave.

(*He resumes walking with his wife, Andal Amma. Darkness. When the lights come dimly on again, they are still walking. Andal Amma takes out the gold cup which she has kept secretly and looks at it. The howl of a fox is heard. Startled, she puts it away again. Kuresar observes her walking with hesitant steps.*)

KURESAR: Why this hesitation? Are you afraid? (*He smiles.*)

ANDAL: Y ... e ... s

KURESAR: One is afraid only when one is carrying a possession.

ANDAL: Yes, I am ...

KURESAR (*looking back, shocked*): Are you?

(*Andal Amma takes out the gold cup and shows it to him.*)

KURESAR: A gold cup? What is it for?

ANDAL: For you ... to drink water from ...

KURESAR: We could have given this too to that poor alms-seeker.

(*He takes the cup from her and throws it away.*)

KURESAR (*smiling*): There is no fear hereafter. Come!

(*He walks on quickly. Andal Amma follows him. Darkness. When the lights come on, Ramanujar, dressed in saffron clothes, is seated at C. Near him is his sister's son, Mudaliyandan. It is morning.*)

RAMANUJAR: Kuresar and his wife Andal Amma are coming to join our *mutt*. Make arrangements for their stay.

(*Kuresar and Andal Amma enter from forestage L. Ramanujar rises, walks towards them and warmly embraces Kuresar.*)

RAMANUJAR (*smiling*): The *tridandam* had come earlier. I was waiting for the *pavitram*.[23] You have come.

KURESAR: What are you saying?

RAMANUJAR: This is my sister's son, Mudaliyandan. He is my tridandam. You are my pavitram. Together, you two are the two central pillars of the edifice of the Vaishnava community. (*Looking at Andal*) Our Vaishnavism needs your keen intelligence too. Man and woman are equal in our society.

(*Andal blushes a little at this.*)

KURESAR (*surprised*): Did you expect our coming here?

RAMANUJAR: If one thinks that affinity will lead to the right of friendship and pave the way for a meeting—do you call that expectation?

(*Kuresar looks at Andal and smiles. The smile indicates that they had indeed mentioned to each other earlier that Ramanujar would be expecting them.*)

RAMANUJAR: I next expect my *Gurunathar*, Yadava Prakasar. When he comes, and if the Merciful One of Kanchi consents, we will all go to Srirangam.

MUDALIYANDAN (*shocked*): Yadava Prakasar? Have you forgotten all the hardship that he caused you?

RAMANUJAR (*stopping him*): No hardship. In any difference of ideology, the first casualty is discrimination. He did not act with any personal animosity towards me. We can see that he is now confused in his mind. All right, you go and make arrangements for these people to stay here. Come, Kuresar. (*He takes them inside.*)

(*Darkness. When the lights come on after a few seconds, Yadava Prakasar stands at C. He could be in his sixties. His face shows distress. The light focuses on him, the rest of the stage is dark. He paces for a while. He is clearly restless.*)

YADAVA PRAKASAR: How much hardship have caused I Ramanujar! Will he now accept me with a cheerful countenance? (*Silence. He paces about again.*) My creed has not given me peace. Was my creed wrong? Or was my understanding of it wrong? (*Silence. He paces about again.*) What will provide support to me who am restless? What is my prop? Who is my prop? Which is right? How should I ask? (*Silence. He paces about again.*) Yes, as Ramanujar says, one should ask, 'Who is the prop?' Only if there is a shape, will it be easy for you to feel it, to hold it. (*Silence. He paces again.*) 'Nirguna Brahmam'. 'The Brahman is attributeless'. That is something I can know, but not feel, nor make others feel. Only if there are attributes, only then the one who enjoys them can say, 'I shall seek no pleasure other than this, even if it is the one that rules Indraloka.'[24] (*Silence. He paces again.*) 'You must accept that Brahmam is the most beautiful form in the universe. Only then will the universe look beautiful.' That was the first lesson that Ramanujar taught me when he was my sishya.[25] How much cruelty I have inflicted on him, refusing to understand that! Will he now accept me?

(*Silence. He paces about again. The lights fade. When they come on after a few seconds, Yadava Prakasar is seated at C. He is asleep. Silence for a while. He wakes up with a start, realizes that he had gone to sleep sitting. He rubs his eyes and looks around. Ramanujar now enters from the corner of forestage L. When Yadava Prakasar sees him coming, he gets up with a start. Ramanujar comes close to him and bows.*)

YADAVA PRAKASAR (*in a startled voice*): What is this? After what I have done to you ...?

RAMANUJAR (*stopping him with a smile*): I knew your doors would always be open for me ... I have entered your house without your permission to take you away.

YADAVA PRAKASAR (*feeling guilty*): Oh Ramanujar, forgive me ...

RAMANUJAR: Sishya forgive guru? What sacrilege ... Let us not waste words any more. Please come, let us go. You represent the farthest bounds of *Advaita*. If you yourself accept my position as right, what more praise can I earn?

(*Yadava Prakasar embraces him. The lights fade. When the lights come on after a few seconds, Tirukkachi Nambi stands facing the audience, his eyes closed and his hands folded in obeisance to the Lord. Enter from L a person about 45 years old. When Tirukkachi Nambi hears him approaching and turns to look at him, his face is at once filled with joy. The visitor is a Vaishnavite. It is morning.*)

TIRUKKACHI NAMBI (*with joy*): Swami, aren't you the Cantor in the Srirangam temple ...?

ARAIYAR: Yes, that is my humble self indeed.

TIRUKKACHI NAMBI: I had the privilege of seeing you in the company of Alavandar. I have heard too about your melodious voice.

(*Enter at this point, Ramanujar, Mudaliyandan, Kuresar, Yadava Prakasar and other disciples. Ramanujar notices Araiyar.*)

TIRUKKACHI NAMBI: This is the Araiyar in the service of the Lord of Srirangam. He has graciously come here from Srirangam.

(*Ramanujar bows to him.*)

RAMANUJAR (*delighted*): Swami, your music and dance are known everywhere. Can't Kanchi Varadan have the pleasure that the Lord of Srirangam enjoys?

ARAIYAR: I have come with the hope that Lord Varadan will grant me the boon that I pray for.

RAMANUJAR: What boon, Swami?

(*Araiyar does not reply, but starts to sing and dance.*)

Pasuram

Eating up all the butter with your little lotus-like hands, then seeing the coir rope being flourished for beating you, your red lips and your mouth—smeared with white curd—curled. The look of fright in your eyes, the cry you feigned, your pleading hands—all this the good Yasoda saw—and wasn't it the limit of her limitless joy?[26]

(*As he melodiously sings and recreates the scene that Kulasekhara Azhwar visualized, he loses himself in dance, causing everyone to stand in rapt attention. As he sings and dances, the temple bell begins to sound slowly and reaches a crescendo as he finishes. The blowing of a conch, then a sudden silence, and then a thunderous voice shaking the very skies.)*

VOICE: Araiyar, we are delighted at the scene that Kulasekhara saw. Varadan will not go back on his word, what do you want?

ARAIYAR: Ramanujar.

(Everyone is shocked, but there is a smile on Ramanujar's face.)

VOICE: Fitting reward for the music. May the One at Srirangam have the joy that I have had. Take Ramanujan to Srirangam.

(Temple bell again. The lights fade.)

ACT II

SCENE 1

(*As the lights come on, we see Ramanujar, middle-aged now, seated at C. Seated in two rows are Kuresar, Mudaliyandan, Kidambi Achan, Periya Nambi, Maraner Nambi, Govindapperumal and a few other disciples. Ramanujar is speaking.*)

RAMANUJAR: A culture built around the temple is the creed of the Vaishnavaite religion. And social justice is its very foundation. Only when temple administration comes into our hands, can the Vaishnavaite society that we visualize take shape.

KURESAR: It is coming.

RAMANUJAR (*not quite comprehending*): What do you mean?

KURESAR: Temple administration.

(*At this point, a Vaishnavaite enters and stands at forestage L Ramanujar notices him.*)

RAMANUJAR (*standing up, delighted*): Please come, Amudanar of Srirangam, now I understand what Kuresar said.

(*Ramanujar embraces Amudanar and leads him to C. Amudanar hands Ramanujar a bunch of keys.*)

AMUDANAR: I gave this bunch of keys to Kuresar yesterday itself. But he asked me to come and hand it to you here today.

(*Ramanujar looks at Kuresar, not comprehending.*)

KURESAR: I had gone to his mother's sradham[27] yesterday.

AMUDANAR: He did not say, 'I am satisfied', whatever I offered him. I asked him what would satisfy him. 'Temple administration,' he said. Then I realized that that was your wish too.

KURESAR: Our new society is going to be built around the temple. And Ramanujar alone can administer it.

AMUDANAR: I understood. So far temple administration has lain with me only in name. I have no strength to control people with selfish interests. In fact, it is I who am satisfied now, Ramanujar. We can now carry out reforms courageously.

(*Ramanujar puts the bunch of keys to his eyes reverentially and sits down.*)

RAMANUJAR: There will be resistance from many quarters. We should learn to swim against the current. But then, there is nothing that we cannot achieve if we have the grace of Alavandar. Lord Arangan commands us in the form of Amudanar. It is our duty to accept the command.

AMUDANAR: Another request ...

RAMANUJAR: Please tell me.

AMUDANAR: From now on, this will be my home. You should grant me that.

RAMANUJAR: That is my good fortune, Amudanar. You are mature in experience of temple management. We need your help. I am sure you know most of the people here. (*Looking at Kidambi Achan*) He is Kidambi Achan. He is my confidant. (*Looking at Govindapperumal*) This is Govindapperumal, my cousin. (*Pointing to Mudaliyandan*) This is my sister's son, Mudaliyandan.

AMUDANAR: The others I know.

RAMANUJAR (*Pointing to him*): Maraner Nambi ...?

AMUDANAR: I know him as one close to Alavandar. I know he belongs to a low caste. Many here didn't like what Alavandar did.[28]

RAMANUJAR: I wish to complete the task that Alavandar began. There will be many more Maraner Nambis in our mutt hereafter. And there will be no taboo against women joining. Temple reform is my first concern. Every day is going to be a temple festival day. And a festival in which people of all castes take part. And the Lord of Srirangam will go in procession through all the streets. There is no high or low before the Divine. The temple sanctum must resound with the hymns of Azhwars alongside the Vedas. The one who has mastered the Tamil Veda as well as the Sanskrit Veda—he alone is the *Ubhaya Vedanti*.[29] We know that the *4000 Prabandhas* reveal newer and newer meanings. Therefore we should not rest content with the interpretations of the elders so far. The bounds of the meaning and import of the Tamil Vedas should extend as far and wide as did the feet of the Lord who measured all the worlds with his stride. And everyone should have the right to offer these interpretations. This is the Vaishnavism that I visualize.

DISCIPLE 1: Everyone has the right to interpret? ... according to his whims?

RAMANUJAR: Interpretation is acceptable if it fits, whoever it comes from. The interpretation offered should satisfy our aesthetic sense. Aesthetics and spirituality are not different from each other. Nor are bhakti and rasa. ... There is still a world of knowledge that I need to acquire. I should seek to know from Ghoshtiyur Nambi the inner meaning of *Ashtaksharam*.[30] That will be my first task. It is also the wish of Periya Nambi.

AMUDANAR: Ghoshtiyur Nambi has locked up in his heart the secret knowledge of Vaishnavism. It is no easy task to make him reveal it.

RAMANUJAR: True effort will always bear fruit.

AMUDANAR: Lord Ranga will shower His grace on us.

(*Darkness.*)

SCENE 2

(*When the lights come on dimly after a few seconds, we see Ramanujar, Kuresar, and Mudaliyandan. They walk round the stage three times. They look fatigued. Ramanujar wipes the sweat off his face. It is early morning.*)

RAMANUJAR (*looking tired*): We have gone round and round. We can't find Ghoshti Purna.

(*At this point a passer-by crosses forestage R to L. Kuresar moves quickly towards him.*)

KURESAR: Swami![31]

(*The passer-by stops.*)

KURESAR: Where is Tirukkhoshtiyur Nambi's house?

PASSER-BY (*Pointing to left*): There. If you go straight and turn right, you will see a small cottage. That is his dwelling place. But he ... he doesn't see anyone ...

KURESAR: Thank you, swami.

(*The three of them walk quickly towards L. After a few seconds, they emerge from R. We now see Tirukkhoshtiyur Nambi sitting on a mat at C, turning over palm-leaf manuscripts. He is in his sixties. It is evident that he leads a strict and disciplined religious life. His face looks hard and severe.*
The three move towards him and stop some distance away from him. He does not notice their coming at all. He is immersed in the palm leaves.)

RAMANUJAR (*very softly*): Swami …

(*He doesn't look up.*)

RAMANUJAR: Swami …

(*Nambi looks up and silently looks at Ramanujar. But it seems as though it has not registered that someone is standing before him.*)

RAMANUJAR: I am Ramanujar, your humble servant. I have come from Srirangam.

(*Nambi continues to look at him.*)

RAMANUJAR (*pointing to Kuresar and Mudaliyandan*): This is Kuresar. He is Mudaliyandan.

(*Nambi keeps looking at Ramanujar without speaking. He seems not to have noticed Kuresar and Mudaliyandan at all.*)

RAMANUJAR: My guru Periya Nambi commanded me to go to you.
NAMBI: What for?
RAMANUJAR: I have taken lessons from many but it is my misfortune that I have not heard the *Rahasyarthas.*[32]

(*Nambi remains silent.*)

RAMANUJAR: You are an ocean of learning. You should bestow your grace on me.

(*Nambi is still silent.*)

RAMANUJAR: I have taken a vow to fulfil an unfulfilled wish of Alavandar. For that it is quite necessary to take lessons from you.
NAMBI: What unfulfilled wish?

RAMANUJAR: It is to find Visishtadvaitic interpretations for the *Vyasasutra*s.[33]

(*Nambi looks him up and down. His look seems to ask Ramanujar if he has the credentials to undertake the task.*)

RAMANUJAR (*understanding*): I am indeed not worthy of undertaking the mission, but you must make me worthy.

NAMBI: All right, we will see later. It is not possible now.

(*He stands up abruptly and leaves. Darkness. When the lights come on dimly again, we see Ramanujar, Kuresar, and Mudaliyandan walking round the stage and stopping, tired.*)

RAMANUJAR (*in a fatigued voice*): Eighteen times we have come. It is the same response each time, 'Come later'! What wrong did I do?

KURESAR: Perhaps he doesn't like our accompanying you?

MUDALIYANDAN: Maybe, if you had gone alone?

RAMANUJAR: I will ask him about that next time we see him. I have an explanation for that too.

(*At this point, a man is seen walking quickly towards Ramanujar.*)

THE MAN: Swami ...

(*Ramanujar turns back to look at him.*)

THE MAN: Nambi calls you.

(*Ramanujar's face brightens. Darkness. After a few seconds, the lights come on and we see, rearstage, Nambi seated on a mat, with palm leaves in his hand. Ramanujar, Kuresar, and Mudaliyandan walk towards him, stand in front, and bow.*)

NAMBI: What did I tell you?

(*Ramanujar looks at him puzzled.*)

NAMBI: You are a *sanyasi*. I asked you to come to take lessons, carrying only your tridandam and pavitram.[34] Why did you bring these people? Is it right to come in a crowd and ask to be taught the Rahasyartham?

RAMANUJAR: Swami, Kuresar is my pavitram, Mudaliyandan my tridandam. I have indeed come the way you wanted me to.

NAMBI: A clever answer, but they shouldn't be here. The lesson is meant only for you.

(*Kuresar and Mudaliyandan leave. Ramanujar at first does not notice their leaving. When he does, he is about to say something, but keeps silent.*)

NAMBI: Shall we start the lesson?

RAMANUJAR: As you wish, Swami.

NAMBI: Come closer.

(*In the dim light, Nambi can be seen to speak, but no sound is heard. This miming lasts two to three minutes. Ramanujar is listening intently. Silence.*)

NAMBI: This Rahasyartham is conveyed only to you. If you communicate it to anyone else, it will be betrayal of the guru and you will go to hell. That is my warning to you. Do you understand?

(*Ramanujar stands silent. Darkness. After a while, the stage is flooded with light. At C is a structure which looks like a temple wall. Ramanujar climbs on to it and stands there. He is flanked by Kurattazhwar and Mudaliyandan. In front of him stand together people of all castes.*)

RAMANUJAR: My purpose is to share my bliss with you. The one who has put on the universe as his body and who permeates the universe is Narayanan. There is no place where God dwells not. If we see Vaikuntam everywhere, there is no high or low in what we see. The four-caste division is an injustice we do to Narayanan. He is *Bhuvanasundaran*, one who has put on the universe as his beautiful form. He is the land that we should reach and He is also the Guide who will take us there. He is our sole haven and refuge. It is our duty to walk the path that He shows. Action! Action! Action! That is our *tarakamantram*.[35] That is the essence of the fruit of what the *Gita* teaches us. Let us lean on Him and march on, with service to society as our supreme mission. Om namo Narayanaya!

(*When he articulates the Narayana mantra aloud, the crowd echoes it. At this moment, Tirukkhoshtiyur Nambi enters from L and rushes towards Ramanujar angrily.*)

NAMBI (*aloud*): This is betrayal of the guru, Ramanujar.

(*The crowd, shocked, turns to look at him.*)

RAMANUJAR (*with a smile*): Please come, gurunatha.

(*He climbs down from the wall and bows to Nambi. Nambi moves a few steps away.*)

NAMBI: What did I say before teaching you the lesson?

RAMANUJAR (*smiling*): You said I was not to communicate the Rahasyartham to anyone else. You also said that if I did, I would go to hell.

NAMBI: And still ...?

RAMANUJAR (*smiling still*): See, gurunatha! There are so many here who have listened to the Rahasyartham and will attain Vaikuntam. Is it a big loss if I alone go to Hell? Should we not rejoice and sing, 'Hail! Hail! Hail! Gone is the curse of existence.'

(*Nambi is silent for a while.*)

NAMBI: You are right. Let us indeed rejoice. Please sing it in full, the song that the Azhwar has composed and left for us, out of his infinite grace.

(*After a few seconds.*)

RAMANUJAR (*sings*):

Pasuram

Hail! Hail! Hail! Gone is the curse of existence. Hell has declined, receded, withdrawn, relented. Yama has no work here anymore, even Kali (Yuga) shall end. Behold, the ocean-hued Lord's spirits have descended on Earth in a host. We have seen them singing and dancing everywhere.[36]

(*The crowd cries out in unison, Om Namo Narayanaya. Nambi embraces Ramanujar tightly.*)

NAMBI: May your name henceforth be *Emberumanar*.[37]

(*The crowd roars in joy. Darkness.*)

SCENE 3

(*The temple bell is heard as the curtain goes up. It is morning. Standing at C are four Vedic Brahmins. They are of different ages—30 to 60—and of different appearances—one quite tall, another very short, one stout, another lean. They are standing in a circle and chatting. While the bell rings, we only see them gesticulating animatedly. We also hear them when the bell stops ringing.)*

BRAHMIN 1: We trusted Alavandar ...

BRAHMIN 2: ... and we were betrayed.

BRAHMIN 3: Did he lose his senses ...

BRAHMIN 4: ... in his ripe old age?

BRAHMIN 1 (*mockingly*): Nice heir!

BRAHMIN 2: How do you expect a fellow from the North[38] ...

BRAHMIN 3: ... to follow the orthodox code?

BRAHMIN 4: He is supposed to be of the Somayaji caste ...

BRAHMIN 1: Who knows?

BRAHMIN 2: How can one born a Smartha ... [39]

BRAHMIN 3: ... become a Vaishnavite?

BRAHMIN 4: They say *Chettikkudi*[40] Nambi was his first guru!

BRAHMIN 1: Tirukkachi Nambi?

BRAHMIN 2: Yes.

BRAHMIN 3: And Periya Nambi ...?

BRAHMIN 4: ... was his next guru. And now Periya Nambi has become a sishya ...

BRAHMINS 1, 2 AND 3 (*together*): ... of the sishya.

(*All four laugh. Brahmin 1 now shields his eyes with his hand and looks towards corner of the stage. Observing him, the others too look in the same direction.*)

BRAHMIN 1 (*in a hushed voice*): It's Periya Nambi ...

BRAHMIN 2: What does he have in his hands ...?

BRAHMIN 3: He is keeping it concealed.

BRAHMIN 4: Shall we follow him?

(*Periya Nambi, holding something covered in his hands, walks looking this way and that. They follow him. They pass through the stage to L. Darkness for a few seconds. When the lights come on, we see someone sitting at C. He is dark-complexioned and looks about 50 years old. He looks ill. He coughs. From his looks it is evident that he is not a Brahmin. His face is emaciated, poverty-stricken.*

Periya Nambi appears at L end of the stage and walks towards him. When he sees Periya Nambi, he rises and walks staggeringly towards him.

Periya Nambi puts his hand on his shoulder and makes him sit again.)

HE: Sacrilege! Sacrilege! You have touched me!

(*The four Brahmins now appear at L of the stage. Standing together, they observe the scene. Their faces show indignation.*)

PERIYA NAMBI: Maraner Nambi! You are Alavandar's sishya. How can you say that? Does caste exist for the true Vaishnavite?

(*Periya Nambi removes the cloth covering, showing three 'vessels' and a 'leaf'. He spreads the 'leaf' on the floor and lays on it 'food' from two of the vessels. The Brahmins exchange angry looks.*)

PERIYA NAMBI: Please eat, it's the *prasadam*[41] of Lord Ranganatha. All diseases will disappear when you take it.

(*The faces of the four Brahmins become angrier when they hear that it is the prasadam of Lord Ranganatha. Maraner Nambi begins to eat and coughs while eating. Periya Nambi takes out a tumbler of water from the third vessel and passes it to him. The cough stops when he drinks the water.*

Now the four Brahmins rush towards C. Startled, Maraner Nambi struggles to rise, but is unable to do so. Periya Nambi motions to him to remain seated. However, Maraner Nambi somehow manages to stand up and move to a corner.)

BRAHMIN 1: Periya Nambi! Is it a case of sishya surpassing guru or guru surpassing sishya?

PERIYA NAMBI: I don't understand.

BRAHMIN 2: What is it that you don't understand? (*Sarcastically*) That great elder there, what caste does he belong to?

VOICE (*suddenly from behind them*): What caste do you and I belong to?

(*They look behind. It is Ramanujar who has spoken. He passes them and goes and stands close to Maraner Nambi. Nambi tries to move away but Ramanujar grips his hand and brings him close to himself.*)

BRAHMIN 3 (*taunting*): Oh Ramanujar, we know nothing about your caste. As for us, we are Brahmins.

RAMANUJAR: I, and he, and Periya Nambi—we belong to the caste of human beings. We know nothing about your caste.

BRAHMIN 4: Are you mocking us?

ATTUZHAY: If you people represent the Brahmin community, then we don't want your contact. That is the lesson that Ramanujar has taught us.

BRAHMIN 1: Such arrogance?

ATTUZHAY: No, such self-confidence. Tomorrow, when the *utsava* idol[51] is taken out in procession, I will demand justice of Ranga.

BRAHMIN 1 (*laughing*): What will you do?

ATTUZHAY: Unless He renders us justice, He cannot take a single step further. That is my vow.

(*The Brahmins stand dumbstruck. Darkness.*

(*When the lights come on, nadaswara*[52] *music is heard from a distance. The music, with the Gambhira Nattai raga being played, comes gradually closer. The chanting of the Veda is also heard. After a couple of minutes enter Attuzhay from L in the rear portion of the stage. She advances to C with her palms spread out as if to stop someone. The nadaswara music is heard even closer and the Veda chanting is louder. Her eyes are fixed on the R of the front stage. As the nadaswara music is heard nearer and nearer, she walks forward with her arms outstretched. Brahmins 1, 2, 3, and 4 enter from right.*)

ATTUZHAY: I will not let you go any further.

BRAHMIN 1 (*angrily*): Are you threatening us?

ATTUZHAY: I am not talking to you.

BRAHMIN 2: Who are you talking to then?

ATTUZHAY: To Ranganatha.

(*The nadaswara music stops.*)

BRAHMIN 3: Are you mad?

ATTUZHAY: Ranga, answer me. These people use your name and insult my father. Is this just?

BRAHMIN 4: It is your father who has insulted the entire community of Brahmins. Ranga's prasadam for a man of the lowest caste? What outrage?

ATTUZHAY: Ranga, tell these people that there is no caste for Sri Vaishnavites. Remind them of the pasuram: Nammazhwar has left for us out of his abundant grace.

(*She sings in a sweet voice.*)

RAMANUJAR: Is that mocking? Then you don't belong to the caste of human beings?

BRAHMIN 1: This man—your guru or sishya—whatever says that the holy water of Ranganatha[42] should go first to the people of the *cheri*. What do you say?

RAMANUJAR: Did he say that? (*He goes and embraces Periya Nambi.*) That would certainly please Ranganatha.

BRAHMIN 2: Ramanujar, even the Lord will not tolerate what you are doing ... a man of low caste ...

RAMANUJAR: Who is of low caste, swami? Wasn't Vyasa,[43] the one who codified the scriptures for us, wasn't he a fisherman? Wasn't the man who told the story of Rama a hunter?[44] People like you pelted stones at Tiruppanazhwar?[45] What happened afterwards?

BRAHMIN 3: Can we equate this fellow with an Azhwar? Pananathar[46] was born bearing an aspect of the Lord of Srirangam. He was an exception to the low caste in which he was born.

RAMANUJAR: It has become your habit to treat what you cannot disown as an exception and thereby to explain away your discomfort. In my scheme of things there is nothing like an exception. It should be the same dharma for everyone—that is my philosophy.

BRAHMIN 4: Why all this futile talk? We are going to excommunicate Periya Nambi. And your preaching is not going to help him.

RAMANUJAR (*smiling*): It is precisely because of my preaching that you have done him this good.

BRAHMIN 1: What good?

RAMANUJAR: That he won't have your company any more. Isn't that a big favour that you have done him?

BRAHMIN 2: Ramanujar, this is sheer arrogance. You are going to pay for it.

BRAHMIN 3 (*angrily*): Come, let us go.

BRAHMIN 4: You will come to know what power we have.

(*They leave in a rage. There is distress on Maraner Nambi's face.*)

RAMANUJAR: You stopped eating halfway. Please finish eating.

MARANER NAMBI: All this trouble for you and Periya Nambi on my account ...

RAMANUJAR: No trouble whatever. Please eat.

(*Maraner Nambi gulps down the food quickly and washes the utensils in water.*)

RAMANUJAR: Maraner Nambi, low self-esteem is a terrible disease. We should shun it.

PERIYA NAMBI: *Udaiyavar*,[47] the caste consciousness which has become part of the blood over generations, do you believe that it will disappear so very easily?

RAMANUJAR: Can we continue to lead a particular kind of life after realizing that it is wrong? Let us strive our best. There should be no regret that we did not try.

(Maraner Nambi looks at Ramanujar with gratitude.)

RAMANUJAR: You don't need to thank me or Periya Nambi. In fact, all the members of the Vaishnavite community are mutually indebted to one another. Come, sing that pasuram, *poliga, poliga …*

(Maraner Nambi sings. There is a wonderful quality to his voice.)

Pasuram

Hail! Hail! Hail! Gone is the curse of existence. Hell has relented. Yama has no work here any more, even Kali (Yuga) shall end. Behold, the apostles of the ocean-hued Lord have descended on Earth in a host. We have seen them singing and dancing everywhere.[48]

(Ramanujar listens with rapt attention. Silence for a few seconds after the song is over.)

RAMANUJAR: 'The apostles of the ocean-hued Lord.' Who are they? We? Or they? *(Points to the direction in which the four Brahmins went.)* It is we … past all doubt, it is we. To make everyone a Vaishnavite, that is the only means to do away with castes. When you cultivate paddy, the grass will automatically disappear. You must from now on teach everyone in this slum to sing the *prabandham*. Lord Ranganathan will then dwell with them.

MARANER NAMBI: Udaiyavar, your words infuse fresh energy and enthusiasm in me. The disease that afflicted me is gone forever. *(He bows to Ramanujar.)*

RAMANUJAR: Come, let us go. Those Brahmins might have gone to your house.

(Darkness for a few seconds. When the lights come on, enter a young woman from R. She must be around 18. She has a pretty face that is also

marked by firmness of purpose. She walks to C carefully looking below, as if to avoid stepping over something. Her face turns red in anger. Hand on her hip, she turns to look behind.)

YOUNG WOMAN: Whose doing is this? Who has spread all these thorny weeds here? Why this boycott call? Lord Ranga, answer me. I am Attuzhay, your devotee and Udaiyavar's *sishyai*.[49] I fear none.

(Enter Brahmins 1, 2, 3, and 4 from front L. Attuzhay does not notice them since she is standing with her back to them. They stand slightly apart. In fact, they had entered when Attuzhay started speaking.)

BRAHMIN 1: Don't ask Ranga. Ask us. We will tell you.

(She turns slowly towards them and looks at them sharply.)

BRAHMIN 2: Your father is turning the slum folk into his kinsmen.

BRAHMIN 3: It is an insult to the *agraharam*.[50]

BRAHMIN 4: The fellow from Kanchipuram is bringing ruin on Srirangam.

ATTUZHAY: Maraner Nambi is a noble Sri Vaishnavite. Food offered to him is food offered to Ranganatha.

(The Brahmins laugh mockingly.)

ATTUZHAY: Why do you laugh?

BRAHMIN 1: From now onwards, you and your father will have your food only in the mansion where Maraner Nambi dwells.

BRAHMIN 2: From now onwards, the Brahmins of the agraharam won't so much as look at you.

BRAHMIN 3: Henceforth you cannot enter the temple either.

ATTUZHAY: I will ask Lord Ranganatha for justice. I will not be cowed down by your threats.

BRAHMIN 1: How will you ask Ranga for justice?

BRAHMIN 2: You can't enter the temple in the first place.

ATTUZHAY: Ranga does not live in the temple alone. He dwells in my heart. He lives in Maraner Nambi's music. We have not imprisoned Ranga in the temple sanctum. For us, the entire universe is God dwelling place. He dwells everywhere in comfort.

BRAHMIN 3: Let Him. We have no objection to that. As for you, Brahmin will defy the taboo that we have decreed and have cor with you.

Pasuram

The Lord of lotus eyes and effulgent form, who is sweet to the heart, and who reclines on the ocean of milk. Those blessed people who worship you—whoever they may be—are my masters, through all lives, behold![53]

The noble souls that Nammazhwar celebrates, are they low in caste? Ranga, ask these people, who created caste, you? ... No, wasn't it these people?

BRAHMIN 1: We did not create caste. Caste is what you attain by virtue of your karma.

(*Attuzhay now confronts them.*)

ATTUZHAY: 'I am the doer of evil deeds, I am their undoer too.' When the Lord Himself has said that, you still talk about the fruits of karma. Is that what all your knowledge of the prabandhas comes to? Is there anyone in your community like Maraner Nambi? You call him a man of the lowest caste? Doesn't your tongue falter in shame? I am the sishyai of Udaiyavar who is gathering everyone into one community and establishing equality among human beings. I ask, Ranga, is this acceptable?

(*At this point three men, evidently not Brahmins, enter.*)

MAN 1: What is wrong with this girl's words?
MAN 2: Did God call people Brahmin and Panchaman?[54]
MAN 3: What a good man Maraner Nambi is! You excommunicated Periya Nambi just because he took food for him?
BRAHMINS 1, 2, 3, and 4 (*together*): Go away! You have no right to speak.

(*Enter Ramanujar at this moment.*)

RAMANUJAR: Why don't they have the right to speak? Any devotee of Lord Vishnu has the right to defy arrogance.
MAN 1: Well said, Swami.
MAN 2: It is not we alone, but (*pointing to R*) all those standing there. All of us are with this girl.
MAN 3: The deity will return to the temple only if the thorny weeds are moved from the front of Periya Nambi's house.

(*The Brahmins look at them angrily.*)

ATTUZHAY: It is not these people who speak. It is Ranga talking through them. Don't you understand even this?

(*There is a commotion in the crowd, heard offstage. The Brahmins look in that direction. Enter two temple priests.*)

PRIEST 1: Attuzhay is right. It is Ranga who speaks through these lowly people. We understood it only now.

PRIEST 2: It was indeed wrong on our part to have listened to these people (*pointing to the Brahmins*) and inflicted cruelty on Periya Nambi. *Udaiyavar*, we realized your might only now.

PRIEST 1: It is only through this girl that we understood the force of your counsel. *Amma*, you were born to rule over us. Periya Nambi is one of us henceforth.

(*He signals with his hand. The nadaswara music is heard aloud. Darkness. When the lights come on, we see Brahmins 1, 2, 3, and 4 and Temple Priests 1, 2, 3, and 4 standing in a row at C. Temple Priests 1 and 2 stand slightly apart, apparently in a posture of explanation.*)

BRAHMIN 1 (*angrily*): You have ruined the code of our community.

BRAHMIN 2: The fellow who sides with pariahs—that fellow has become all important for you?

BRAHMIN 3: You go and support that haughty girl?

BRAHMIN 4: Go and build a temple in the cheri for Ranganatha. That will make it complete.

(*Priests 1 and 2 smile.*)

BRAHMIN 1: What are you smiling about?

PRIEST 1: Yesterday all those men were on the side of that fellow from Sriperumpudur. What else could we have done?

PRIEST 2: If the deity had remained in the street all night, whose disgrace would it have been?

PRIEST 1: There is another way to deal with Ramanujar.

PRIEST 2: A final, decisive way.

BRAHMIN 1: What way?

PRIEST 1: Have patience.

BRAHMIN 2: The Vaishnavism that we Brahmins have cherished and preserved ...

BRAHMIN 3: ... is now the common property of the whole village.

BRAHMIN 4: Pariahs and men of low castes have become Brahmins now.

BRAHMIN 1: We trusted Alavandar ...

BRAHMIN 2: ... and were betrayed.

BRAHMIN 3: Did he become senile ...

BRAHMIN 4: ... in his last days?

PRIEST 1: Don't be in a hurry.

PRIEST 2: There *is* a way. (*After a while*) We deliberately put on that playacting yesterday.

BRAHMIN 2: What way is there?

PRIESTS 1 and 2: A decisive, final way.

(*They approach Brahmin 1 and whisper something into his ears. Brahmins 2, 3, and 4 move closer and listen too. The faces of all four brighten.*)

BRAHMIN 1: We feared that you too had gone over to the side of Udaiyavan.

BRAHMIN 2: Sacrilege!

BRAHMIN 3: Nice plan, good idea.

BRAHMIN 4: So the law of Manu will not die.

SCENE 4

(*When the curtain goes up, the stage is flooded with light. We hear the noise of people moving about in the street. There is also the sound of nadaswara music. After a few seconds, enter from L a man and a woman. The woman is fair-complexioned and beautiful. The man is tall, dark, broad-shouldered, and looks like a warrior. He is holding an umbrella over the woman's head to protect her from the sun's heat. He is casting a loving look at her all the time. As they go round the stage once and reach R end, enter from L Ramanujar and two disciples. The disciples look at the couple in wonder. There is a smile on Udaiyavar's face. The couple does not notice Ramanujar and his disciples and they exit from R.*)

DISCIPLE 1: Who is that crazy fellow, holding an umbrella for a woman?

DISCIPLE 2: You see, his goddess's lovely body shouldn't get charred by the scorching heat. That is why.

DISCIPLE 1: You mean darkened like his own body? (*Both of them laugh. Udaiyavar looks at them angrily. The disciples bow their heads.*)

RAMANUJAR: Which is black—your minds or his complexion?

(*Silence.*)

RAMANUJAR: He knows how to love. Do you know who he is?

DISICIPLES 1 AND 2: No.

RAMANUJAR: He is Urangavilli,[55] the bodyguard of King Akalanga Chola. That is his wife, Ponnachi. He worships beauty. Is that wrong?

DISCIPLE 1: W ... i ... f ... e? (*He drawls out the word.*)

RAMANUJAR: Beauty is beauty—whether it belongs to a wife or to Ranga. This woman has inner beauty as well as outer charm. Go call them here. I want to talk to them.

(*As they talk, soft nadaswara music continues to be heard. The disciples exit R. Udaiyavar pensively paces the stage for a few seconds. At this moment, the Araiyar of Sri Ranganatha temple enters from L and walks quickly towards Ramanujar. Ramanujar smiles at him.*)

RAMANUJAR: Araiyar, why this hurry?

ARAIYAR (*tense / excited*): Udaiyavar, ... yesterday ... (*He falters and breaks into tears.*)

(*Ramanujar puts his hand on his shoulder and smiles.*)

ARAIYAR: Is it true, Swami?

RAMANUJAR (*smiling*): The Divine doesn't as yet want to take me to Himself. The attempt of the temple priests failed.

(*He closes his eyes. Darkness. After a few seconds, gentle blue light on the stage. We see Ramanujar standing near R corner of the back portion of the stage. He sings.*)

Pasuram

Open the door, Nappinnai, daughter-in-law of the mighty Nandagopala, the possessor of great elephants. O lady with fragrant locks of hair, see, the cock crows, song birds of many feathers chirp sweetly on the Madhavi bower. O lady with slender fingers clasping a ball, come with your lotus-hands, with bangles jingling softly, and open the door, that we may sing your lord's name.[56]

(*When he finishes singing, enter a middle-aged woman, with infinite sadness in her face and a vessel in her hand. There is a smile on Ramanujar's face. As the woman presents alms to Ramanujar, her hands tremble and her eyes moisten.*)

RAMANUJAR: Why do you look so sad? Any problem at home ...?

(*She is first silent and then bursts into tears. Unable to speak, she abruptly scurries back indoors. Not understanding, Ramanujar keeps looking in the direction in which she went and then looks at the rice she has left in the alms-bowl in his hands. He then picks up a little of it, smells it, and closes his eyes in distress. Periya Nambi, who now enters and approaches Ramanujar, is bewildered at seeing Ramanujar standing distressed with eyes closed.*)

PERIYA NAMBI: Udaiyavar, why thus ...

(*Ramanujar points to the alms-bowl. Periya Nambi looks at him not comprehending.*)

RAMANUJAR: Poisoned food. This is another plot by the temple priests to kill me. The lady of the house couldn't go through with it. She rushed back in after making her tears bear witness.

PERIYA NAMBI (*quite disturbed*): But why this plot?

RAMANUJAR: The temple priests must have planned it even the other day when your daughter Attuzhay stopped the deity Ranganatha's procession. I suspected as much and now my suspicion is confirmed. Well, I love this life and don't want to die so easily. (*Smiles.*)

(*Darkness. When the lights come on, we see Ramanujar and Araiyar standing as before. Ramanujar opens his eyes.*)

ARAIYAR: The priests who dared to make the attempt on your life have run away from the place. It is only now that we know the reason they fled.

RAMANUJAR: What is the reason?

ARAIYAR: Guilty consciences.

RAMANUJAR (*stopping him*): They were not very honest people. They have appropriated temple property. The proof of that is in my possession. And now they were scared that they will face punishment for murder too along with the other crime. That is why they have run away.

(*Enter from R Disciples 1 and 2, Urangavilli and Ponnachi.
Urangavilli and Ponnachi pay their respects to Ramanujar, touching his
feet. Ramanujar raises Urangavilli with his hand.*)

RAMANUJAR (*smiling*): Where is the umbrella?

URANGAVILLI: It is not so hot now.

PONNACHI: I don't like his holding an umbrella for me. But I am unable
to stop him, O Udaiyavar.

RAMANUJAR: Why stop him? You can't issue a decree against love.
Urangavilli is simply one who worships beauty, isn't that so?

URANGAVILLI: Yes.

RAMANUJAR: You have never seen anything as beautiful as Ponnachi?

URANGAVILLI: No, and such beauty cannot exist anywhere else.

RAMANUJAR: Come with me, I'll show you.

(*Urangavilli looks at Ponnachi.*)

PONNACHI: Please go with him. Udaiyavar will only do you good.

RAMANUJAR: You too come. Araiyar, please come too.

(*Darkness. After a few seconds, as the lights reappear, we see the image
of Lord Ranganatha in silhouette at the rear portion of the stage, while at C
stand Ramanujar, Urangavilli, Ponnachi, and Araiyar taking darshan[57]
of that image.*)

RAMANUJAR: Look there. Look at Ranga's eyes, small as lotuses but
deeper than the sea. Look at His coral-red mouth, His blue frame.
Oh, oh, what a sight, how wonderful! Like the blue ocean aflame,
the lotus eyes, the face, the *Sudarsana Chakra*![58]

(*Ramanujar looks at Araiyar who then begins to sing. The sound of
temple bells.*)

Pasuram

The dark-hued lord is the one who came as a cowherd and stole and
ate butter. He, the lord of Srirangam, is indeed the lord of all gods.
He has stolen my heart. The eyes which have beheld him—will they
behold aught else?[59]

(*Urangavilli stands in rapt attention. His eyes grip Ponnachi's hands
tightly. There are tears of joy in Ponnachi's eyes.*)

RAMANUJAR: It is *Bhuvana Sundara*[60] who permeates the universe and manifests as the universe. (*Silence for a while.*) The universe holds such great beauty, if we only know how to love it. (*Silence.*) If only we realize that we are the universe, there is no room for any exclusion. Urangavilli, your universe which was narrow so far— does it appear large and wide now?

URANGAVILLI (*opening his eyes*): Yes, Swami.

(*Urangavilli bends low to touch Ramanujar's feet. Ramanujar stops and raises him.*)

RAMANUJAR: Right, come, let us go.

(*Darkness. After a few seconds, as the lights come on, enter Ramanujar from the rear with his hand on Urangavilli's shoulder. Araiyar and Ponnachi are standing close to them. Disciples 1 and 2 enter from front R. Ramanujar and his company do not notice the disciples but exit through L.*)

DISCIPLE 1: Why is Udaiyavar acting thus?

DISCIPLE 2: I don't understand either.

DISCIPLE 1: Should he touch the body of a warrior of low caste after having a bath?

DISCIPLE 2: There is more. Did you see him before he went to the Kaveri to bathe?

DISCIPLE 1: Then his hand was placed on the shoulder of the Brahmin Kuresar.

DISCIPLE 1: After the bath ...

DISCIPLE 2: ... his arm on the *Marava's*[61] shoulder!

DISCIPLE 1: It looked as though they were returning from the temple.

DISCIPLE 2 (*looking to right*): There, Udaiyavar is coming back alone.

DISCIPLE 1: Let us ask him about this.

DISCIPLE 2: Hasn't he told us that we can put questions to him about anything?

DISCIPLE 1: Isn't it his policy that there should be no inhibitions?

DISCIPLE 2: Hasn't he declared that questioning is the beginning of knowledge?

(*Enter Udaiyavar. The disciples bow to him. He places his hands on their shoulders and smiles.*)

DISCIPLE 1: Udaiyavar, we have a doubt.

RAMANUJAR: Is it about our philosophy?

DISCIPLE 2: No. Your hand rested on Kuresar's shoulder before bathing in the Kaveri.

DISCIPLE 1: After the purification by the bath in the river, you placed your arm on Urangavilli's shoulder.

DISCIPLES 1 AND 2: This is what we fail to understand.

RAMANUJAR (*smiling*): I now understand that you have not understood our philosophy either.

DISCIPLE 1: We understand the philosophy, Swami. *Chit, achit,*[62] God ...

RAMANUJAR (*stopping him*): Enough ... What you haven't understood is that life and philosophy are not two different things. Well, I have no time now. I will explain it to you later ...

(*He exits. The disciples keep looking in the direction in which he left. Darkness ... After a few seconds, when the lights come on, we see the disciples standing with a torn* veshti[63] *in their hands and looking very angry.*)

DISCIPLE 1: What an outrage. Who has torn this veshti into bits?

DISCIPLE 2: We shouldn't let him go unpunished, if we can catch him.

DISCIPLE 1: Rascal.

DISCIPLE 2: Rogue.

DISCIPLE 1: Envious fellow.

DISCIPLE 2: And a new veshti at that ...

DISCIPLE 1: Who will make good the loss?

(*Enter Udaiyavar from left.*)

DISCIPLE 1 AND 2 (*excited and angry*): Our veshti ...

RAMANUJAR (*stopping them*): Yes, I heard you as I came here. I understand your anger. We will find out about it later. Now, you must do something for me.

DISCIPLE 1 (*slightly disappointed*): What?

(*Silence.*)

DISCIPLE 2: Please tell us what it is.

RAMANUJAR: Tonight both of you must go to Urangavilli's house and ...
(*Pauses.*)

DISCIPLE 1: ... and ...?

RAMANUJAR: When Ponnachi is asleep you must steal the ornaments that she is wearing and bring them to me ...

DISCIPLES 1 AND 2 (*shocked*): Steal her ornaments? What are you saying, Udaiyavar?

RAMANUJAR: Don't you understand ?

DISCIPLES 1 AND 2: Well, what about Urangavilli ...?

RAMANUJAR: Oh, is that your problem? Have no fear. He is away on duty as Akalanga Chola's bodyguard. He returns late tonight. Before that you should go and ...

DISCIPLES 1 AND 2: Why should we steal those things?

RAMANUJAR: Well, if you don't want to do it ...

DISICIPLES 1 and 2: All right. We'll do it.

(*Darkness. After a few seconds, there is dim light and we see Ponnachi lying on her side, asleep. After a while, enter from back L Disciples 1 and 2 tiptoeing towards her.*)

DISCIPLE 1 (*in a hushed tone*): She is asleep.

DISCIPLE 2 (*remaining in the back left corner, also in a hushed voice*): All right, I will stand guard here and see if anyone comes. You go and ...

DISCIPLE 1(*in a lamenting tone*): What a dilemma ...

DISCIPLE 1: Careful! ... Don't wake her up ...

(*Ponnachi has sensed their entry and their hushed talk. But she is lying still. Disciple 1 goes near her and removes the bangles from her hand carefully. Disciple 2 stands watching the entrance. Ponnachi slowly turns to the other side. Disciple 1, scared, begins to run. Seeing him flee, Disciple 2 runs away too. Ponnachi sits up and smiles. Darkness. When dim light returns, we see Udaiyavar lying down. Disciples 1 and 2 run towards him. Hearing them run towards him, Udaiyavar sits up. Disciple 1 hands him the bangles.*)

DISCIPLE 1: It is done.

RAMANUJAR: Tell me in detail.

DISCIPLE 2: Well, I stood guard. He took away the bangles from her hand. She turned to lie on the other side. We ran away.

RAMANUJAR: You shouldn't have hurried. Go back, watch what is happening there now and come back and tell me ...

DISCIPLES 1 AND 2 (*hesitating*): Go back?

RAMANUJAR (*in a stern voice*): Yes.

(*Udaiyavar lets them give no answer and lies down again. The disciples leave reluctantly. Darkness.*

When dim light returns, we see the two disciples at the back L corner and Urangavilli and Ponnachi at C. Urangavilli appears quite angry.)

URANGAVILLI: And you turned to the other side?

PONNACHI: Only in order that they might take the bangles from the other hand too. Poor wretches ...

URANGAVILLI (*interrupting her*): You told yourself, 'These are *my* bangles. *I* will give them to another.' And this pride of possession, this arrogance, scared them off.

PONNACHI: What are you saying?

URANGAVILLI: Your pride drove them away.

PONNACHI (*remorseful*): The fault was mine, Swami. Humility cannot be taught. It has to develop spontaneously.

> *(The disciples leave. Darkness.*
> *It is morning light when the lights come on. Enter Ramanujar from front L. Araiyar is with him. The two disciples rush from front R, fall at Ramanujar's feet and hold them tight. There is a realization of guilt on their faces.)*

RAMANUJAR: What happened? Get up.

DISCIPLES (*together*): We tried to see you even last night. But you had gone to sleep.

RAMANUJAR: What is the matter?

DISCIPLE 1: Last night, when we went back to Urangavilli's place, he was chiding Ponnachi.

DISCIPLE 2: He was saying that we were scared away by her egoistic pride which made her act with the feeling 'This is *my* possession, *I* am giving it.'

DISCIPLE 1: What a noble soul he is!

RAMANUJAR (*sarcastic*): A Marava!

DISCIPLE 2: Forgive us, Udaiyavar!

RAMANUJAR (*sarcastic*): You are Brahmins!

> *(Disciples 1 and 2 stand shamefaced.)*

RAMANUJAR (*sarcastic still*): It was wrong on my part to walk with my hand on the shoulders of a Marava after having a bath.

> *(Silence.)*

RAMANUJAR: You of the purest breed of Brahmins—how angry you were with someone who had torn an ordinary veshti!

(*Silence.*)

RAMANUJAR (*with a smile*): So it was the veshti which brought out your enlightened philosophy.

(*Silence.*)

RAMANUJAR (*smiling still*): The man who tore your veshti is a rogue, rascal, an envious fellow. (*Pause.*) Those who have realized the *Brahman* rave and rant and curse on account of a torn veshti. But a Marava rebukes his wife for not giving away her gold ornaments without pride of possession. Do you at least see now who indeed has realized the Brahman?

(*Silence.*)

RAMANUJAR: Have you at least realized now that in the community of Vaishnavites there is no Brahmin and no Marava?

(*Enter at this moment Urangavilli and Ponnachi. The two disciples prostrate at the feet of Urangavilli. He is taken aback and he looks at Ramanujar, who smiles. Araiyar begins to sing.*)

Pasuram

What though they study the six Angas, and the four Vedas, rank ahead of all, and pride themselves on their Brahmin lineage. If they but speak ill of your devotees, that very moment, they decline and become veritable Pulaiyas, O Lord of the great city of Srirangam![64]

(*Darkness.*)

SCENE 5

(*Darkness for a few seconds as the curtain goes up. When the lights come on, enter from front L Ramanujar, Kidambi Achan, Kuresar, Mudaliyandan, and two other disciples. In the background, a pasuram of Tirumangai Azhwar is being poured out in musical form. Listening to the music in rapt attention, Ramanujar and the others are walking slowly. It is morning.*)

Pasuram

The lord resides in the hearts of sages of great austerities, and in
Venkatam (Tirupati) where rises high the fragrant smoke of *akhil*, burnt
by foresters. He came here as a beautiful Vedic lad. Like the thoughts
of the *deva*s, O heart, you too have entered into His service sweetly.[65]

RAMANUJAR: There! ... the fragrant smoke from akhil wood That is
the sign to let us know that we have arrived at *Tiruvenkatam*. This
place, which has been hallowed by the feet of the Azhwars is indeed
Vaikuntam itself. Our disciples Yagnesan and Varadan live here in
Ashtasahasram. Let us go first to the dwelling of Varadan.

(*They walk round the stage twice. As they go round for the third time,
they stop at L end of the front stage. Kidambi Achan sheilds his eyes with his
hand and looks towards R end.*)

KIDAMBI ACHAN: There is a small cottage there. It might be
Varadan's ...

RAMANUJAR: Yes, come let us go there.

(*They walk towards the cottage and stop a few feet before it.*)

KIDAMBI ACHAN (*softly*): Swami!

(*Silence.*)

KURESAR: Perhaps nobody's in.

KIDAMBI ACHAN (*advancing a little farther and looking*): It looks as though
someone is in. Swami!

FEMALE VOICE: Who do you want?

KIDAMBI ACHAN: Udaiyavar and his disciples have come. Isn't Varadan
at home?

FEMALE VOICE (*delightedly*): Oh, please come, please come. Varadan is
not at home, but you should not go away. Udaiyavar, you should
honour me by coming in. But ... (*hesitating*)

RAMANUJAR: Tell me, Amma, don't hesitate.

FEMALE VOICE: I am your disciple's wife.

RAMANUJAR: And your name is Paruttikkollai, I know.

FEMALE VOICE (*showing surprise*): Is there nothing that Udaiyavar does
not know?

RAMANUJAR: I also know Varadan's poverty-stricken state. Go on.

PARUTTIKKOLLAI (*hesitates*): How can I see you with a torn upper cloth ...

(*Ramanujar removes the parivattam[66] from his head and throws it in.*)

RAMANUJAR: You can wear this and see us.

(*She comes out after a few seconds. She is an extremely beautiful woman. She bows to Udaiyavar and the others.*)

PARUTTIKKOLLAI: How can I thank you for understanding my embarrassing position and helping me out?

RAMANUJAR (*to the others*): Varadan is a Brahmin by birth and a Vaishnavite by conviction. This girl is not a Brahmin by birth, but she too is a Vaishnavite by belief. That was sufficient reason for the two of them to get married. (*Smiling*) Am I right, Amma?

(*She blushes deeply.*)

RAMANUJAR (*to the others*): You too should witness the nobility of their conjugal life. Today, we will have our food in their house.

PARUTTIKKOLLAI (*delighted*): Swami, it is a great privilege for me.

RAMANUJAR: All right, we will return after having a bath. Won't Varadan also be back by then? Come, let us go.

(*They leave. Paruttikkollai's brow is lined with worry as she is lost in thought. The lights are focused on her face while the rest of the stage is dark.*)

PARUTTIKKOLLAI'S VOICE: There isn't even a grain of rice at home. My husband has gone for alms but what he brings won't suffice even for the two of us. But what could I have done when Udaiyavar himself said that they would return for food. Hmm. What can I do now? (*Silence. And then a moment's joy as a sign that an idea has struck her, but that is succeeded immediately by an expression of distress.*) Is it right to do that? Is love a matter of the body or the heart? If my husband will understand me, why should I care for the others? Yes, I must do so.

(*Darkness. When the lights come on after a few seconds, we see at C of the rear portion of the stage, a middle-aged merchant, seated, resting his body against cushions. He is sitting on a silk mat, with a thick gold chain round*)

his neck, glittering rings on his fingers, and a silk upper cloth wrapped round. The lights are focused on him while the rest of the stage is dark. He is lost in thought.)

MERCHANT'S VOICE: What use is all my wealth? She refused to so much as look at me. And she says that emaciated *Parpan* who lives by alms would do for her! She rejected me and went and married that worthless Parpan![67]

That Parpan's luck! He gets this *Sridevi*![68] And I get Sridevi's elder sister ...! (*Sighs.*)

(*Brooding thus, he tilts his head and looks inside, then closes his eyes. Darkness. When the lights come on after a few seconds, we see Paruttikkollai standing at the left corner of the front portion of the stage. She stands looking at the sleeping merchant for a while.*)

PARUTTIKKOLLAI: Ayya ...

(*The merchant half-opens his eyes and when he sees Paruttikkollai he wakes up with a start, rubs his eyes, and looks at her again.*)

MERCHANT: Do I dream?

(*He rubs his eyes once again and then stands up.*)

PARUTTIKKOLLAI: This is no dream. It's real.
MERCHANT (*moving close to her*): How come ... you are ... here?
PARUTTIKKOLLAI: I have come to beg ...

(*The merchant is astonished. He looks at her quizzically.*)

MERCHANT: You ... come to beg ... I don't understand.
PARUTTIKKOLLAI: I want some grocery items. I have some unexpected guests.

(*The merchant is silent.*)

PARUTTIKKOLLAI: Please show mercy.
MERCHANT (*with a smile*): Do you know the price you have to pay for this?
PARUTTIKKOLLAI: Yes, I do.

(*The merchant is taken back. Silence for a few seconds.*)

PARUTTIKKOLLAI: First, give me the things. I will go fulfil my duties as a hostess and then come back and pay the debt.

MERCHANT: Your husband, that Parpan ...

PARUTTIKKOLLAI: He will understand ...

MERCHANT: How can I trust you?

PARUTTIKKOLLAI: You just have to. What else can I say?

MERCHANT (*gripping her hands*): All right. I'll send the things to your house with my servant ... (*In a pleading voice*) Don't deceive me.

PARUTTIKKOLLAI (*releasing her hands*): Paruttikkollai will not break her word.

(*Darkness. When the lights come on after a few seconds, we see, in R corner of the rear portion of the stage Ramanujar, Kuresar, Kidambi Achan, Mudaliyandan, and the disciples standing. They are wiping their wet hands as a sign of having eaten the feast. Paruttikkollai and Varadan are also standing, with their faces full of joy.*)

KIDAMBI ACHAN (*pleased*): Excellent cooking ... I have eaten my fill.

RAMANUJAR: Varadan, all praise to you. You should be proud that you have got such an excellent wife owing to the grace of the Lord of Tirupati.

(*Varadan looks proudly at his wife.*)

KURESAR: Amma, shouldn't you find out about Kidambi Achan's culinary skills?[69] You must both visit Srirangam.

KIDAMBI ACHAN: Kidambi Achan's culinary skills? What chance do they have against cooking like this? I am only praying to the Lord of Tirupati that after this Udaiyavar doesn't dismiss me from his service.

(*Everyone laughs.*)

RAMANUJAR: All right. ... We will get along. We will have darshan of the Lord and return to Srirangam.

(*They exit through the left end of the front portion of the stage. After seeing them off, Varadan comes and stands close to his wife. Silence for a few seconds.*)

PARUTTIKKOLLAI: Why are you silent?

VARADAN: I don't understand at all. How did you manage to get up a feast like this? There wasn't even a grain of rice at home. Did Udaiyavar himself supply the things?

PARUTTIKKOLLAI: Please let us go in. I'll tell you.

(*They go in. Darkness. When the lights return, we see the merchant pacing up and down in a yard. There is anger on his face.*)

MERCHANT (*angrily to himself, pacing up and down*): It looks as though she has deceived me.

(*Silence. He paces the yard.*)

MERCHANT: I should have supplied the grocery items only afterwards. I am a fool.

(*At this point, Varadan and Paruttikkollai enter and stand at L corner of the front stage. The merchant, startled, looks at them both. They walk towards him.*)

VARADAN: The master of the house must himself repay the debt he has incurred. I have brought you the price of the things you supplied. Please accept it.

MERCHANT (*shocked*): What are you saying?

VARADAN: Well, you can take only her body as the price for what you gave. Not her heart. That already belongs to me. So you may copulate with her like copulating with a corpse in the dark. I have no objection to that.

(*The merchant, still shocked, stands still.*)

PARUTTIKKOLLAI: We provided a feast to Ramanujar. It was your help which made that possible. The price that we are paying for the great privilege of feeding Ramanujar is quite petty. Isn't it just this body that you want? Please take it.

(*She advances towards the merchant. He, however, moves towards the rear portion of the stage and stands at C with his back to them.*)

VARADAN (*turning to go*): All right, let me take leave, Ayya.

MERCHANT (*in a steady but hoarse voice*): Please take Amma and go. Please go away.

(*Darkness. When the lights come on after a few seconds, we see Ramanujar and one of his disciples standing. Ramanujar is listening to the disciple who is reporting something.*)

DISCIPLE: ... This is what happened. The merchant sent Varadan and his wife back. Will God forgive that rogue?

(*Ramanujar stands silent.*)

RAMANUJAR (*after a while*): Go, bring him to me.
DISCIPLE: Who, Varadan?
RAMANUJAR: No, the merchant.
DISCIPLE (*taken aback*): The merchant?
RAMANUJAR: His basic decency has still not deserted him. He is worthy of becoming a true Vaishnavite.

(*Darkness.*)

SCENE 6

(*The lights are focused on the C of the stage. Seated at the back are Ramanujar and near him Kuresar and Andal Amma. We see them as shadow figures. In the lighted portion in front are two disciples in conversation.*)

DISCIPLE 1: Udaiyavar has been dictating for quite a long time today. And Kuresar has been writing it down. Who is to go and tell them that it is getting late for food?
DISCIPLE 2: If it is a matter of writing a commentary on the *Brahmasutras*, where is the room for hunger and food?
DISCIPLE 1: But don't we need to provide our own stomachs with food? How can we eat unless Udaiyavar eats?
DISCIPLE 2: Why is Andal Amma also sitting there?
DISCIPLE 1: It seems Udaiyavar said that she should be with them when this is being done.
DISCIPLE 2: Why?
DISCIPLE 1: Why? That lady has verily mastered all the *sasthras*.[70] She is a wife truly worthy of her husband.
DISCIPLE 2: Is that so?
DISCIPLE 1: Not only that ... if they have a difference of opinion with Udaiyavar, both of them have a right to express it. It seems Kuresar said to Udaiyavar even before starting to write, 'If the views you express are not acceptable to me at any time, I will immediately stop writing'!

DISCIPLE 2: Only Kuresar can say that.

DISCIPLE 1: Why, you can say that too. Udaiyavar has granted that right to all of us. But ...

DISCIPLE 2: But ...?

DISCIPLE 1: You and I won't say it.

DISCIPLE 2: Why not?

DISCIPLE 1: Well, you and I know how much we know ...

(*Laughing, they exit through the L end of the front portion of the stage. The entire stage is lit up now. Kuresar is taking down what Ramanujar dictates.*)

RAMANUJAR: Chit. That is, the soul. Achit. That is, the body. Both are the attributes of God. Just as a flower possesses both fragrance and colour. Just as the sea consists of both waves and the waterdrops that make up the waves. When the Upanishads say, 'No it isn't, it isn't, it isn't',[71] what they mean is 'It is not as these attributes alone that Brahmam exists'; they do not mean that Brahmam has no attributes. Therefore, *Nirguna Brahmam*[72] is not an acceptable concept. If you say that a clay pot is an illusory manifestation of clay, it can only mean that the pot cannot exist without clay. If you say that the entire universe is an illusion, it can only mean that the universe cannot exist without God. Therefore, the doctrine of *maya* is not acceptable. Even though chit, achit, and God are all basically one, chit and achit have existence in so far as they are God's attributes. They are not merely illusory appearances. God represents the frontiers of all meaning. And our life is a journey towards that end. Chit, that is the soul, can know everything. The soul is consciousness turned wholly on itself.

(*When Ramanujar says this, Kuresar stops writing. Andal sees this and smiles, but does not say anything. Ramanujar has not noticed that Kuresar has stopped writing and continues to dictate.*)

RAMANUJAR: The body is mere lifeless matter. When I say, 'I see this', the object that is seen acquires the special marked attribute of 'what is seen'. But what 'sees' is not the body; 'seeing' is merely the consequence of the existence of the body in accord with the soul. Wisdom lies in assimilating objects in the outer world to one's own experience. It is by means of wisdom, which mediates between the inner consciousness and the outer world, that we see objects, feel them, experience them.

(It is only at this point that Ramanujar notices that Kuresar is not writing.)

RAMANUJAR *(a little surprised)*: Why aren't you writing?

ANDAL: In accordance with our agreement.

RAMANUJAR: What agreement?

ANDAL: Your view is not acceptable to him.

RAMANUJAR *(appearing slightly annoyed)*: Which view?

KURESAR: Shall I read out the last sentence I have written down?

RAMANUJAR: If you do ...?

KURESAR: You will understand that the view that you expressed after that point is not acceptable to me.

RAMANUJAR *(slightly angry)*: Is this a riddle? Say directly what you want to say. Which view?

(Saying this, Ramanujar abruptly gets up.)

RAMANUJAR: All right, you don't have to write any more.

(Ramanujar leaves.)

ANDAL: You could have told him straight?

KURESAR: He should be aware of the continuity of thought. This is a matter on which I cannot compromise.

(At this point, Disciple 1 enters and walks up to them.)

DISCIPLE 1: Udaiyavar invites you to come and eat.

KURESAR: No food for me till the completion of the portion which Udaiyavar was dictating.

(Disciple 1 goes in. A few seconds after he leaves, enter Ramanujar.)

RAMANUJAR: What has this got to do with food?

KURESAR: So fas as I am concerned, the time for feeding my stomach has not arrived yet.

(Ramanujar goes and sits in his place. Silence for a few seconds.)

RAMANUJAR *(with a smile)*: Andal Amma, you please tell me. What mistake did I make?

ANDAL: Do I have leave to say it as a riddle?

RAMANUJAR: Please do.

ANDAL: If the small one is born in the womb of the dead one, what will it feed on and where will it dwell?[73]

(Ramanujar contemplates this. After a few moments, his face brightens. He gets up, raises Kuresar, and embraces him.)

RAMANUJAR: The mistake was mine. Please forgive me.

KURESAR: You must forgive me too. I spoke harshly.

RAMANUJAR: It was indeed wrong of me to say, 'The soul has the attribute of knowing everything. The soul is consciousness centred on itself'. When the soul has no existence independent of the Divine, it was indeed a mistake for me to talk of 'consciousness centred on itself'. It was a contradiction in terms. Is that right, Andal Amma?

(She smiles.)

RAMANUJAR: All right ... What next ...

ANDAL: Food for the stomach. We shouldn't incur the sin of having starved Udaiyavar.

RAMANUJAR: Well, I shouldn't incur the sin of having starved you.

(Darkness.)

ACT III

SCENE 1

(*When the lights come on, we see, at C of the forestage, four or five elderly Vaishnavite Brahmins standing and in conversation. It is morning.*)

BRAHMIN 1: If things go on like this, there will be no Brahmins left after a few days.

BRAHMIN 2 (*with mocking laughter*): Everyone is a Vaishnavite!

BRAHMIN 3 (*sarcastic*): This is Enlightenment according to Ramanujar.

BRAHMIN 4 (*sarcastic*): The pariah quarters will be our Vaikuntam.

BRAHMIN 1: Ramanujar's name and fame have spread all over the Chola as well as Pandiya country.

BRAHMIN 2: Why won't they, if he turns everyone into a Vaishnavite, no matter what caste he belongs to?

BRAHMIN 3: We hear that in the Pandiya country many a Saivite has become a Vishnu devotee.

BRAHMIN 4: It seems that Ramanujar has made even Panchamas wear the sacred thread?[74]

BRAHMIN 1: They say that at Tiruppulingudi in the Pandiya country, this fellow Ramanujar prostrated at the feet of a Panchama woman.

BRAHMIN 2: It seems she cited a quotation from *Tiruvaimozhi!*[75]

BRAHMIN 3: The administration of the Srirangam temple is now in his hands.

BRAHMIN 4: And there is festivity, dance, song, and celebration every day!

BRAHMIN 1: Not only in the Big Temple,[76] in all the Vishnu temples in the Chola and Pandiya countries all days are festival days!

BRAHMIN 2: And feasting by all castes sitting together.

(*Enter from L forestage four or five Saivites. From their appearance, they do not look like Brahmins. They have sacred ash on their foreheads[77] and all over their bodies.*)

BRAHMIN 1 (*noticing them, in a low voice*): Saivites?

(*The Saivites approach the Brahmins.*)

BRAHMIN 1: Welcome, welcome, *Namah Sivaya Namaha!*[78]

SAIVITE 1 (*surprised*): What, you too have joined us?

BRAHMIN 2(*with a smile*): Well, what do we do? Ramanujar says we are not true Vaishnavites. Naturally, *Panchaksharam*[79] is our only refuge now.

SAIVITE 2: But then, the only sound heard all through the Chola and Pandiya countries now is your *Narayana mantram!*[80] .

BRAHMIN 1: That is what we were talking about. We must stop Ramanujar.

BRAHMIN 2: It can be done if you people put your mind to it.

SAIVITE 1: We?

SAIVITE 2: What can we do about it?

BRAHMIN 3: If you do not stop Ramanujar now, all Siva temples will turn into Vishnu shrines.

BRAHMIN 4: And Panchamas will perform ritual puja in all of them.

SAIVITE 3: But aren't you Vaishnavites now?

BRAHMIN 1: We are Vaishnavites, but we are not allowed to enter the temple of Lord Ranganatha. That is Ramanujar's decree.

SAIVITE 4: Why ...?

BRAHMIN 2: Because we don't accept his leadership.

BRAHMIN 3: And there are many like us.

BRAHMIN 4: Do song and dance constitute spirituality?

SAIVITE 1: What shall we do to stop him?

BRAHMIN 1: Let us go and complain to the Chola king.

BRAHMIN 2: It will be good for us if he is banished.

BRAHMIN 3: And Vishnu and Siva will both be at peace.

BRAHMIN 4: Religion and spirituality will survive.

BRAHMIN 1: Let us take the help of Naluran and chalk out a plan of action.

SAIVITE 2 (*surprised*): Naluran? But he is Kuresar's disciple? How do we chalk out a plan with his help?

BRAHMIN 3: The Chola minister Naluran was once betrayed like us.[81] What he is doing now is playacting!

BRAHMIN 4 (*with a smile*): It is a plot he has hatched to find out what is happening at the Ramanuja mutt.

BRAHMINS 1, 2, 3, 4 AND SAIVITES 1, 2, 3, 4 (*together*): Let us go see Naluran today itself and devise a plan.

(*Darkness.*)

SCENE 2

(When the lights come on after a few seconds, the Chola king is ensconced on a decorated seat at C of the rear portion of the stage. Naluran is standing respectfully in front of the king. His face indicates that he is middle-aged and full of guile. He must have communicated something to the king who is lost in thought. It is morning.)

KING: You are saying that even Vaishnavites oppose Ramanujar.

NALURAN: Your Majesty, they say he is the enemy of Vaishnavite dharma.

KING: Why ...?

NALURAN: Your Majesty, how can the country be governed if someone says king and beggar are the same? Or, what comes to the same thing, that there is no difference between Parpanan and Panchaman?

KING: Does Ramanujar say that?

NALURAN: Well, it is to find out what happens in his mutt that I pretended to be Kuresar's disciple.

KING: Well, you are saying that both Vaishnavites and Saivites are Ramanujar's enemies. Isn't that so?

NALURAN: Yes.

KING: What do you want us to do about it?

(The king rises and paces the hall.)

NALURAN: Lord Siva is the god that the majority of our countrymen worship. He is the prime deity of the Chola country.

KING: But we have devotees of Vishnu too in our country. Aren't you yourself a Vaishnavite?

NALURAN: If Ramanujar grows in strength, all Siva temples will become Vishnu shrines. Please tell me, Your Majesty, do we want the writ of followers of Narayana to run in the temples that Rajaraja Chola built? I am a Vaishnavite, it is true, but I seek the welfare of the entire country.

(The king silently paces the hall.)

KING: What do you want us to do?

NALURAN: If Ramanujar signs a declaration saying, 'There is no god above Lord Siva' ...

KING: If he does …?

NALURAN: When the leader says that, the disciples will automatically accept it. Saivism will triumph. What more do we want?

KING: Will the people accept this?

NALURAN: The triumph of Saivism will be the triumph of Saivites, won't it? If Ramanujar himself accepts Siva as the supreme god, then the Vaishnavite party will split into two. And it is certain that Udaiyavar's influence will decline.

KING: What if Ramanujar refuses to sign such a declaration …?

NALURAN: We will banish him.

(*The king, silent again, paces the hall.*)

KING: All right, fetch Ramanujar here. We will discuss the matter with him and take a decision.

(*Exit the King. Naluran stands for a while seeing him leave. He then claps his hands. Enter a palace guard.*)

NALURAN: Call the Army Chief here.

(*Exit the guard. Naluran, thoughtful, paces the hall. Enter the Army Chief.*)

NALURAN: The king has ordered Ramanujar to be arrested and brought here.

(*The Army Chief hesitates.*)

NALURAN: It is His Majesty's command. And it is your duty to carry it out.

ARMY CHIEF: His Majesty never asks for anyone to be arrested without reason. … That is what I am wondering.

NALURAN: There is reason. This is a confidential matter of the state. Hmm. Do at once what you are told.

(*The Army Chief still stands there, quite reluctant. It is clear from his countenance that he has no love for Naluran. Darkness.*)

SCENE 3

(*When the lights come on, we see an aged Kuresar standing at C of the forestage. Standing near him are Periya Nambi, also quite aged now, and*

Disciples 1 and 2. Enter a man who walks very quickly from L end of the forestage to C.)

THE MAN: Ayya ... Kuresar?

KURESAR: Yes, it is I.

THE MAN (*hesitating*): It is quite a confidential matter.

KURESAR: You can speak. These are my close friends..

THE MAN: The Army Chief sent me on this secret mission. Naluran has betrayed you. Palace guards are on their way here to arrest Ramanujar and take him to the palace. Ask him to flee. I am leaving.

(He goes away quickly. Kuresar, Periya Nambi, and the disciples stand dumbfounded.)

KURESAR (*to Periya Nambi*): I will put on Udaiyavar's saffron robes and go with the guards. You must ask Udaiyavar to leave the mutt through the secret passage.

PERIYA NAMBI: Let me too come with you. (*Looking at the disciples.*) These people will explain the matter to Udaiyavar.

KURESAR: Should you, at this ripe old age ...?

PERIYA NAMBI: Don't stop me. (*To the disciples*) Go quickly and tell Udaiyavar to put on ordinary white clothes and leave this place and the Chola country altogether. Quick. Go.

(Exit disciples 1 and 2. Kuresar too leaves through L end of the forestage. As soon as he leaves, the guards enter from L.)

GUARD 1: We must see Ramanujar.

PERIYA NAMBI: He is taking a bath.

GUARD 1: It is the king's command that we should immediately arrest and take him.

PERIYA NAMBI: Arrest him? What offence did he commit?

GUARD 1: We don't know. We have just come to carry out the king's orders.

PERIYA NAMBI: I will go in and fetch him.

(He leaves through R end of the forestage.)

GUARD 1: Why have they ordered us to arrest a sanyasi and bring him along? I don't understand.

GUARD 2: It appears to me that the Army Chief too doesn't quite like this.

GUARD 3: This could be a plot by Naluran.

GUARD 1: Is there anyone who likes Naluran?

GUARD 2: The Army Chief has commanded us to bring Ramanujar with the utmost respect.

(*Silence for a while.*)

GUARD 3 (*peeping in*): Where is he?

(*Enter Kuresar, clad in saffron robes, and Periya Nambi.*)

KURESAR (*with a smile*): Am I such a dangerous character, that I should be arrested?

(*The guards bow to him.*)

GUARD 1: The Army Chief has ordered us to bring you with full security. The palanquin is waiting outside.

KURESAR (*surprised*): Palanquin, whatever for?

GUARD 2: We have to reach *Gangai Konda Cholapuram.* Can you walk that distance?

KURESAR: I can walk. But this aged swami ... for him perhaps ...

PERIYA NAMBI: I can walk.

KURESAR: All right. Let us go in the palanquin. His Majesty should not get a bad name for ordering me to be arrested and taken along. If we walk, we will be inviting everyone's attention. Come, let us go.

(*They exit through the L of the forestage. Darkness.*

When the lights return after a few seconds, Disciples 1 and 2 are standing at C. One of them has a piece of white clothing in his hand. Enter Ramanujar, now in his late sixties, from L end of the rear portion of the stage. He has just had a bath and his clothes are wet. Though he is old, his frame shows no signs of ageing. He notices the white clothing in the disciple's hand.)

RAMANUJAR: Who is this for? Where is my robe?

DISCIPLE 1: This is for you. The king's guards came to arrest you at his command.

(*Ramanujar, shocked, stands still.*)

DISCIPLE 2: Kuresar has put on your saffron clothes and has gone with the guards calling himself Ramanujar. He has asked you to wear this white clothing.

(*Ramanujar keeps standing, still shocked.*)

DISCIPLE 1: He has told us to ask you to escape through the secret passage and leave the Chola country altogether.

(*Enter at this point Kidambi Achan, Mudaliyandan, and Andal Amma.*)

KIDAMBI ACHAN: Yes, please go. The very future of Vaishnavism lies in your escaping now as Kuresar has asked you to. Please don't delay.

ANDAL AMMA: He asked me too, when he left, to urge you to escape capture and to leave at once.

KIDAMBI ACHAN: I'll make all arrangements for our journey.

RAMANUJAR: Where is Periya Nambi?

DISCIPLE 1: He too has gone with Kuresar.

RAMANUJAR: At this ripe old age, he goes courageously with Kuresar. And I must run away?

ANDAL AMMA: But you are not just an individual. You are an institution.

RAMANUJAR: I still don't understand. What did they come to arrest me for?

ANDAL AMMA: Even when Kuresar accepted Naluran as a disciple, I had a suspicion that it was a conspiracy. I told Kuresar so, but he didn't listen.

MUDALIYANDAN: Time is running out. Shall we start?

RAMANUJAR: Andal Amma, take care of the mutt. If we must leave the Chola country, we need to travel north-west. (*Silence for a while.*) I think this must be a conspiracy hatched by the Vaishnavite Brahmins who hate us. (*Silence.*) All right. This is Ranganatha's command. Let things take their course. We will cross the Kaveri and move westwards to the Nilgiris. Our friend Nallan Chakravarti lives there. Do you know how he got that name?

MUDALIYANDAN: Please, let us start, Swami.

RAMANUJAR: He once performed the funeral rites for a Panchama. The Brahmins of the village excommunicated him for that act. But the Lord said to him then, 'You may be a bad man for the community, but to me you are a good man.'[82] Let us seek shelter with that good

man. Come, let us start. Lord Ranganatha will protect Kuresar and
Periya Nambi.

(*He takes the white clothing from the disciple and exits through the right
end of the rear stage.*)

KIDAMBI ACHAN: Andal Amma, I hope we will be able to keep in touch
with one another, with the grace of Ranganatha. We will send
someone to find out what befell Kuresar and Periya Nambi. Om
Namo Narayanaya.

(*Darkness.*)

SCENE 4

(*When the lights come on, we see the Chola king ensconced in a decorated
seat. Near him is Naluran. Standing a little away on both sides are
Vaishnavite Brahmins and Saivites. Standing in front are Kuresar in saffron
robes and Periya Nambi, surrounded by guards. It is morning.*)

NALURAN: Your Majesty, a mix-up has taken place, owing to mistaken
identity.

KING: I don't understand.

NALURAN: You ordered them to fetch Ramanujar. These fools have gone
and brought this man.

KURESAR: Well, I told them I am Ramanujar, so they brought me here.

NALURAN (*mocking*): Can a devotee of Ramanujar tell a lie?

BRAHMIN 1: It is only the devotees of Ramanujar who tell lies. A true
Vaishnavite won't.

KURESAR: If so-called 'true Vaishnavites' are like you and Naluran, even
Lord Narayana will grow sceptical about saving and protecting all
human beings.

BRAHMIN 2 (*angrily*): Your Majesty, this man is insulting us.

KING: Was it right on your part to come here posing as Ramanujar?
Who are you?

KURESAR: One may utter a falsehood if some good will come of it. That
is what the Tamil scripture says. My name is Kuresan.

KING: Where is Ramanujar?

KURESAR: He is not in the Chola country now.

NALURAN (*wild with anger*): Has he run away?

KURESAR: Are you saying that he should have come here to the royal court just to find out for himself how many ungrateful wretches there are in the Chola country?

NALURAN: Your Majesty, he is insulting you. He is saying that everyone here is an ungrateful wretch!

KING: Where has Ramanujar gone?

KURESAR: He might have gone to seek to live with good people.

(The king rises from his seat, walks past those standing and paces the hall thoughtfully. Silence for a while.)

KING *(to Naluran)*: Naluran, Ramanujar has himself left the country. So what is the problem now? Wasn't it your plan to banish him?

NALURAN: This man has abetted Ramanujar's escape. Impersonation is his second offence. He must be punished for both.

SAIVITE 1: Why not take from this man the declaration that you were planning to take from Ramanujar? Where is that palm leaf?

NALURAN: That is a good idea.

(He takes out a palm leaf from the folds of his clothing. He turns to call a guard who brings a stylus.)

NALURAN: Kuresar, you must sign on this palm leaf. You too, Periya Nambi.

KURESAR: What is it?

NALURAN *(reads)*: '*Siva paradharam nasti*' (There is no god greater than Siva).

(Kuresar takes the palm leaf and the stylus in his hands. He writes something on the leaf and returns it to Naluran. Naluran's face flushes in anger. He moves towards the king.)

NALURAN *(livid with rage)*: What insolence! Your Majesty, he is insulting us.

KING: What is the matter? Be calm and tell me.

(Naluran reads out what Kuresar has written.)

NALURAN: *Dronam asti tatah param.*

KING: Please explain that.

(The rage felt by the Saivites shows in their faces.)

NALURAN: Your Majesty, you know that *sivam* also means a unit of measurement. You also know that *dronam* refers to a measure that is larger than sivam. Kuresar is quibbling, saying, 'Dronam is a larger measure than sivam'.

SAIVITE 2: Your Majesty, the Saivites of this country will not tolerate this insult.

SAIVITE 3 (*angrily*): Your Majesty, this is the same man who said, 'When there is Lord Vishnu who will grant you all joy, why do you need Siva, the god that haunts the cremation ground?'

SAIVITE 4 (*angrily*): Your Majesty, how can we tolerate this mocking equation of the Spirit that moves the entire universe with a mere unit of measurement?

KING: How do you want us to deal with him?

NALURAN: If we have the eyes of both these men gouged out, we can bring round to our path all those who owe allegiance to them now.

BRAHMINS 1, 2, 3, 4 AND DAIVITES 1, 2, 3, 4 (*together*): Excellent decision. The entire land will approve of it.

KING (*reluctantly*): Do it if you feel it is the right thing. But the blame will not attach to me.

(*The king leaves the court. After his departure, Naluran walks close to Kuresar and looks at him with eyes full of hatred. Silence for a while.*)

NALURAN: Our village temple used to be under the control of my ancestors. It was your Udaiyavar who wrested it from my father's management twenty years ago on charges of corruption. I was waiting to have my revenge. The bird I wanted has fled. (*In a louder voice*) And you are responsible for his flight. (*To the guards*) Pluck out this man's eyes and throw them away.

KURESAR: In fact, I myself wanted to suggest this to you.

NALURAN (*angrily*): What?

KURESAR (*with a smile*): That my eyes should be gouged out for the sin of having looked at you.

NALURAN (*furious*): Drag them away and blind them. Hmm.

(*He walks away angrily ... Darkness.*

After a few seconds, we see at the rear of stage, two fierce-looking soldiers with dense moustaches, each holding a burning torch in his hand. There is no other light on the stage except that of the two torches. Standing in front are Kuresar and Periya Nambi, each with his hands held tight behind his back by two other soldiers. The soldiers holding the torches move slowly step by step towards Kuresar and Periya Nambi.

   As they come very near and move the torches close to the eyes of the two men, with the speed of lightning Kuresar and Periya Nambi swiftly extricate their hands, snatch the torches out of the soldiers' hands, and hold the torches themselves to their own eyes. The soldiers, who had not expected this at all, look at the burnt faces of the two men and scream in eerie fright. Hearing their scream, Naluran walks in quickly from L end of the rear stage ...)

NALURAN: What happened?

SOLDIER 1: They burnt their own eyes out with the torches.

NALURAN (*to Kuresar and Periya Nambi*): Don't you, even now, regret being Ramanujar's devotees?

KURESAR: If our regret is going to afford you joy, we regret that we cannot provide you that joy.

NALURAN (*mad with rage*): Take them away and dump them somewhere beyond the village limits.

   (*The soldiers drag the two men away. Darkness.*
   Dim light after a few seconds. Kuresar and Periya Nambi, holding each other's hands, move slowly round the stage twice. They now have pieces of cloth tied around their eyes.)

PERIYA NAMBI (*stopping*): Oh Kuresar, I can't take even a step further.

   (*He sits down.*)

KURESAR: We are at *Pasupati Koyil.*[83]

PERIYA NAMBI: So what? I can hardly breathe. (*He speaks haltingly.*) Our Father is calling me.

KURESAR: Swami, please try to draw just a little more strength from Him and move on. Let us reach Srirangam and ...

PERIYA NAMBI: Please sit. (*Kuresar sits down too. Periya Nambi now lies down placing his head on Kuresar's lap.*)

PERIYA NAMBI (*in soft and halting tones*): What greater blessing can a true Vaishnavite wish for than to lie down on another Vaishnavite's lap and reach *Tirunadu*? Let my last rites take place only here ...

KURESAR (*intensely moved*): Swami, let us reach Srirangam and ...

PERIYA NAMBI: Have you forgotten what Udaiyavar used to say ... for a true Vaishnavite every place that he sets eyes on is Vaikuntam.

Pasupati Koyil is a holy shrine too. It was from here that Nathamuni and Kuruhai Kavalappan reached Tirunadu.[84] Your lap is my Vaikuntam.

(He closes his eyes. Kuresar realizes that he is dead. Two soldiers enter at this moment. Hearing the sound of their feet, Kuresar looks up at them.)

SOLDIER 1: The Army Chief sent us here. He has commanded us to give you any help that you need.

(Kuresar is looking silently at Periya Nambi.)

SOLDIER 2: Is he dead?

(Kuresar nods. The soldiers look at each other. Silence for a few seconds.)

KURESAR: His funeral rites must be performed right here. That was his last wish. After that, I must reach Srirangam. Please convey my gratitude to your Army Chief.

(Soldier 1 looks towards L end of the front stage and gestures to someone, asking them to come in. Enter two more soldiers.)

SOLDIER 1: Make arrangements here to perform the last rites for this swami. After that *(pointing to Kuresar)*, escort him safely to Srirangam. This is our Army Chief's command and it is to be carried out with secrecy.

KURESAR: Is your Army Chief a Vaishnavite?

SOLDIER 2: No, Ayya, he is a Saivite.

KURESAR: Naluran is not a Vaishnvite ... he was only born in a Vaishnavite family. That was just an accident. Your Army Chief, born in a Saivite family, is a true Vaishnavite!

SOLDIER 2: 'To be a good human being—that is the greatest religion'. That is what our Army Chief says often, Ayya.

(Kuresar looks up at him. Silence for a few seconds.)

KURESAR: You are right. If Ramanujar had been here, he would certainly have liked to meet your Army Chief. All right. Let us see what is to be done next.

(He struggles to rise. The soldiers help him to do so. Darkness ...)

SCENE 5

(*The scene is set in a forest. In the dim light, we see some figures moving carefully step by step. We hear the cries of animals. Four or five shadowy figures go round the stage twice. As they are walking round for the third time, enter from L forestage four other men with lit torches in their hands. They are tough men of the forest. As they come in, the shadowy figures seen earlier, who are now to the R, notice them and stop, startled. The men who have come in have bows and arrows in their hands. They appear to be hunters.*)

HUNTER 1(*in a loud, threatening voice*): Who are all of you?

(*As the hunters move closer, we recognize the shadowy figures to be Ramanujar, Kidambi Achan, Mudaliyandan, and disciples.*)

RAMANUJAR: We come from the Chola country. We seem to have lost our way.

HUNTER 1: Who did you come looking for?

RAMANUJAR: We came looking for a good man we know. From your appearance, you too seem to be good people.

HUNTER 1: What is the name of the person you came to see?

RAMANUJAR: Nallan Chakravarti.

(*Hunter 1 looks at the other hunters and smiles.*)

RAMANUJAR: He ... used to live here ...

HUNTER 2: Well, he has reached Tirunadu.

HUNTER 3: He was our guru.

HUNTER 4: He was the one who taught us good ways and enabled us to show ourselves to be good human beings to people like you.

HUNTER 1: Who are you?

KIDAMBI ACHAN (*pointing to Ramanujar*): He is your gurunathar's gurunathar, Ramanujar.

(*The hunters at once prostrate themselves before Ramanujar.*)

HUNTER 1: Our gurunathar used to tell us about you ever so often, how you are creating a new society.

HUNTER 2: It was our gurunathar who uplifted us from a very base state to a state of dignity.

HUNTER 3: He was a pure and holy man who performed the last rites even for Panchamas.

HUNTER 4: We are all Vaishnvites, Ayya.

MUDALIYANDAN: We have come here unable to bear the persecution in the Chola kingdom.

HUNTER 1: Is that so? You are all very tired. You must first have food … but … we are hunters, Panchamas.

(*Ramanujar moves close to him and tightly embraces him.*)

RAMANUJAR: Can a disciple of Nallan talk like this? Who is high and who is low among Vaishnavites? Come, let us have food first and then chalk out our next plans.

(*The hunters, Ramanujar, and others exit through L forestage.*
When the lights return, it is morning. The hunters, Ramanujar, and others are seated on a mat at C. The hunters are on one side and the others on the other. They are in conversation.)

HUNTER 1: There is a Lord Narasimha temple at Tondanur.

HUNTER 2: Tondanur Nambi looks upon you as his guru, although he has never seen you in person.

HUNTER 3: He is a relative of our gurunathar.

HUNTER 4: And there is Melukote, which is situated near Tondanur.

HUNTER 1: You must certainly visit that place.

HUNTER 2: The king of Tondanur is a Jain.

HUNTER 3: His name is Bittaladevan.

HUNTER 4: There are eight thousand Jain ascetics in that kingdom.

HUNTER 1: All of them proud and haughty.

HUNTER 2: And they simply have the king under their thumb.

HUNTER 3: The queen is a very good soul.

HUNTER 4: Her name is Chandala Devi.

RAMANUJAR: Why do you want me to go there?

HUNTER 1: The music of Narayana's name must be heard there.

(*Ramanujar smiles looking at his followers.*)

HUNTER 1: I'll send a good number of our men with you to ensure your safety.

RAMANUJAR: I need your help in another important matter.

HUNTER 1: Please command us …

RAMANUJAR: One of my disciples must go to Srirangam with a couple of your men as escorts. I wish to have vital information about the developments there.

HUNTER 1: They can leave right away today.

(*At this moment, a man enters from L, moves quickly towards Hunter 1 and whispers something into his ear. The face of Hunter 1 brightens. He rises and leaves with the man but immediately returns leading a person, a Vaishnavite who appears about 50 years old. The other hunters rise and bow to him.*)

HUNTER 1: Oh Udaiyavar, this is Tondanur Nambi.

(*Tondanur Nambi, his face radiant, bows to Ramanujar.*)

TONDANUR NAMBI: I never expected the privilege of seeing you, least of all in this Nilgiri forest. ... Oh, the grace of Lord Narayana!

RAMANUJAR: We must thank the Chola kingdom for this!

TONDANUR NAMBI: I don't understand.

RAMANUJAR: Well, we'll talk about that later. We are now going with you to Tondanur.

TONDANUR NAMBI (*delighted*): It is indeed my good fortune.

RAMANUJAR: Your king is a Jain, isn't he?

TONDANUR NAMBI: Yes, he is a good man. There is a way to see him.

RAMANUJAR: What way?

TONDANUR NAMBI: The princess, his only daughter, is possessed by a spirit. You must agree to drive that spirit away.

MUDALIYANDAN: Didn't the Jains try to do it themselves?

TONDANUR NAMBI: They did, without success.

(*Ramanujar is thoughtful.*)

TONDANUR NAMBI: I will talk to the queen and arrange to take you to the palace.

RAMANUJAR: You say she is possessed by a spirit. What does she do? How does she behave?

TONDANUR NAMBI: She rolls down her dense hair, shakes her head violently, and dances round and round, laughing hysterically. She is a very good-looking girl, just about 18.

HUNTER 1: Ayya, there is nothing that is impossible for you. You must accomplish this.

KIDAMBI ACHAN: For the sake of Vaishnavism.

RAMANUJAR: All right, we will make an attempt.

(Instantly, there is a chorus chanting of Om Namo Narayanaya. Darkness.)

SCENE 6

(When the lights come on, we see king Bittaladevan pacing the stage. His wife, Chandala Devi, is telling him something. The king seems to be pondering over what she has told him. He looks about 50 years old, not very tall and his face looks serene. The queen is around 40. Her countenance indicates her maturity. It is morning.)

BITTALADEVAN: What is the name of this Vaishnavite ascetic?

CHANDALA DEVI: Ramanujar.

(Silence. He paces the stage again.)

BITTALADEVAN: Does Tondanur Nambi believe he can cure our daughter?

CHANDALA DEVI: Yes, he does.

(Silence. He paces the stage again.)

BITTALADEVAN: Will our Jain gurus approve of this?

CHANDALA DEVI: Why should we bother whether they will or won't approve? Our daughter must be cured. That is all there is to it, isn't it?

(Silence again. He paces the stage for a while.)

BITTALADEVAN: No king can rule this country having antagonized the religious leaders. This is politics and you don't understand it.

CHANDALA DEVI: I don't care for politics. My only concern is our daughter must get well.

(Silence again for a while as he paces the stage.)

BITTALADEVAN: Are they here?

CHANDALA DEVI: Yes, shall I call them in?

(The King nods. Chandala Devi exits through L end of the forestage. The King paces the stage again. Enter, after a few seconds, Chandala Devi,

Tondanur Nambi, and Ramanujar. Bittaladevan looks at them uncertainly.
A hesitant smile appears on his face.)

BITTALADEVAN: Welcome, welcome.

(*Saying so, he bows to them.*)

BITTALADEVAN: Swami, are you confident that you can cure my
daughter?

RAMANUJAR: I am not saying that I can. But I am confident that there
is nothing unachievable for Narayanan, the god I worship.

BITTALADEVAN (*startled*): Narayanan?

RAMANUJAR: Yes, not even an atom can move unless He wills it.

BITTALADEVAN: That is the problem.

RAMANUJAR: What is the problem?

BITTALADEVAN: Our religious leaders will not approve of this.

RAMANUJAR: Well, they could have cured her.

BITTALADEVAN: They ask, 'How else could karma work itself out?'

RAMANUJAR: Karma is only a rationalizing device in the sophistry of
cause and effect. The Divine is the cause and He is the consequence.
If we surrender to Him, what place has karma then? The One who
accepts responsibility will also resolve all issues. The one and only
path that we suggest is the path of prapatti.[85]

BITTALADEVAN: Prapatti?

RAMANUJAR: Prapatti is the goal of all bhakti. Anyway, we can engage
in this philosophical inquiry later. Please tell me about your
daughter's affliction.

CHANDALA DEVI: She has been possessed by a spirit for the last three
years. No medicine, no magic has worked.

RAMANUJAR: Did this happen all of a sudden?

BITTALADEVAN: Three years ago, my enemies invaded this country all
of a sudden. They ravaged this land. There was no crime that they
did not commit. The havoc they caused entering the palace and the
ladies' chambers—it is all too shameful even to recount. Seeing no
other way out, I rescued my country and my rule by parting with
a finger.

RAMANUJAR: Finger? I don't understand.

(*Bittaladevan moves close to Ramanujar and shows his right hand to*
him. The little finger is missing from it.)

BITTALADEVAN: They demanded it from me as acknowledgement of their sovereignity. Well, I gave it. But from then onwards, my daughter Neela Devi has been afflicted with this disease.

RAMANUJAR (*surprised*): Neela Devi is her name?

BITTALADEVAN: Why?

RAMANUJAR: Well, that is the name of one of Krishna's friends at *Gokulam*.[86]

BITTALADEVAN: I have kept my daughter confined in a small room. She ...

RAMANUJAR (*shocked*): Kept her confined in a small room? That is very wrong.

BITTALADEVAN: What else could we have done? It was getting intolerable.

RAMANUJAR: Take her out of that prison and leave her in the palace garden. There should be nobody else in the garden.

BITTALADEVAN: She is uncontrollable. Such aggressive impulses and such demonic power she has.

RAMANUJAR: Well, that will be my problem. Just do as I said. I will come back tomorrow morning.

(*Bittaladevan looks at Chandala Devi. Her face seems to show her faith in Ramanujar's ability to cure her daughter. Exit Ramanujar and Tondanur Nambi. Darkness.*)

SCENE 7

(*When the lights reappear, we see the 18-year-old Princess Neela Devi, seated at C. Her long hair is open and spread. She is sitting cross-legged, her head bowed and touching the earth. Her face is not visible. Silence for a few seconds.*

Ramanujar enters from L end of the forestage. He notices her as soon as he enters.

Silence.

He now moves near and stands in front of her. Neela Devi very slowly lifts her head. Now her hair falls on both sides of her face, on her shoulders. She does not seem to have noticed Ramanujar.

And then, suddenly, her head starts shaking furiously, with her hair flying around. After a few moments she stands up abruptly and dances. It is a violent whirl of a dance, reminding one of the mythical dance of Fate. And there sounds the beat of a small drum in the background. Her dance lasts for quite a few minutes and then stops. And now we hear her voice from the background, as though recorded.)

VOICE: The Goddess *Kali*, the Goddess who strikes terror in the hearts of evil men, the one who destroys wrongdoers, who crushes and hurls away all lust-possessed men—I am that She, I am that She, I am She ...

(The sound of her weird laughter, 'Ha, ha, ha, ha', is heard.
She dances again in fury and agony. Dancing and dancing, her body tires and at last she stands still. She then notices Ramanujar. She looks at him hard and long.)

NEELA DEVI (*in a low voice*): Who are you?

(Ramanujar moves closer, but she draws back.)

NEELA DEVI: Don't come near me.

RAMANUJAR (*smiles*): Look around you, look at this lovely flower garden. Here is the Divine revealing Himself as Nature, blossoming and dancing as hundreds and hundreds of flowers of all hues. (*He spreads out his hands to show her.*)

NEELA DEVI: Who are you?

(Ramanujar quickly moves round the stage and points out to her all the flowers in the garden.)

RAMANUJAR: Jasmine, *iruvatchi, champak, vengai, asoka* ... When the world around you is so lovely, why are you alone, so full of fury?

(Neela Devi silently looks at all the flowers that he is pointing to. He picks a jasmine and brings it to her.)

RAMANUJAR: Is there anything like the fragrance of jasmine? (*He stretches out his hand.*) Come, smell it. (*He holds it close to her face.*)

(She steps back a little.)

NEELA DEVI: I am ... I am ... afraid ...

RAMANUJAR (*smiling*): Fear is the demon that possesses you. That is what fills you with fury as though in self-defence. Just take in the fragrance of this jasmine and you will be all right.

(*At this moment, the strains of a flute are heard. It is melodious music, soft and sweet, wafting through the air and melting the heart.*)

RAMANUJAR: Look! Listen! This flower garden has now turned into *Brindavan*[87] itself, Neela Devi! Here is Krishna Himself playing the flute. You know what Periazhwar says? He says that when Krishna played the flute, the entire universe stood still.

(*He sings.*)

Pasuram

His little fingers ran over the holes, his red eyes turned, his lips formed like a bud, little beads of sweat stood over his eyebrows. When Govinda brought his flute and played on it, hosts of birds left their nests and lay like broken twigs all around. The cows spread their legs and lay down with lowered heads and motionless ears.[88]

(*Neela, overwhelmed by the song, continues to stand in rapt attention when the song is over and is followed by the strains of the flute. The music stops. Silence.*)

NEELA DEVI: Who are you, Swami?

RAMANUJAR: The Lord's servant, your saviour.

NEELA DEVI (*smiles sadly*): The saviour who arrived too late!

RAMANUJAR: All the experiences that befall us are holy, Neela Devi. They are pathways to knowledge of the Divine.

(*Neela Devi is unable to control her sobs. Ramanujar goes near her and touches her shoulder.*)

RAMANUJAR: Come, let us go see your parents. They must be anxious to see you.

(*Darkness.*

When the lights return, we see Bittaladevan and Chandala Devi in their royal seats at C of the rear stage. Tondanur Nambi is standing before them. Ramanujar and Neela Devi enter from L of the forestage. Neela Devi has tied up her hair. The king and the queen rise happily, move towards their daughter, and hug her. They look gratefully at Ramanujar.)

BITTALADEVAN: Swami, I am at a loss as to how I can express my gratitude to you.

CHANDALA DEVI: You have verily given us back our life.

(*Neeela Devi's eyes brim with tears.*)

BITTALADEVAN: This is an astounding achievement, Swami.

RAMANUJAR: It is all His grace. He makes everything happen at the appropriate time.

(*Enter at this moment the chief of the Jain ascetics. He is astonished to see Neela Devi behaving normally. He looks alternately at the king, the queen, and Ramanujar.*)

BITTALADEVAN: Ramanujar has cured my daughter, Swami.

JAIN CHIEF (*sarcastic*): Through some magic mantra?

RAMANUJAR: Yes, it is the Ashtakshari mantra, Om Namo Narayanaya.

JAIN CHIEF: What kind of plot is this?

RAMANUJAR: No plot whatsoever.

TONDANUR NAMBI: An achievement, on the contrary. What you could not do, my guru accomplished. It is Narayanan's grace.

JAIN CHIEF: I can't believe it.

CHANDALA DEVI: Here is my daughter standing before you, cured of her affliction. What do you mean, you can't believe it. (*To her husband*) Please come, let us be seated.

(*They resume their seats.*)

CHANDALA DEVI: We are at a loss as to what we can do for you in grateful return. His Majesty will grant whatever you want. You have our word for it.

(*Neela Devi goes and stands beside Chandala Devi.*)

JAIN CHIEF (*in a slightly mocking tone*): Was it the Narayanaya mantra that cured you?

NEELA DEVI: I recovered the confidence that I had lost. The one who gave it back to me is that Swami. (*Points to Ramanujar.*)

JAIN CHIEF: The spirit has fled ?

NEELA DEVI: The spirit that had possessed me was fear. The one who drove it away is that Swami. (*Once again, she points to Ramanujar.*)

JAIN CHIEF (*to Ramanujar, in a sarcastic tone*): Did your god drive it away?

RAMANUJAR: There is nothing like my god and your god. There is only one God. It all depends on our vision.

JAIN CHIEF: And, pray, what may your vision be?

RAMANUJAR: We don't make the Divine into a subtle form, invisible to the eye, and put that form away, segregated, in a nowhere land. Our God manifests Himself as a human and raises the human to the Divine state. That is the secret of all *avatars*.

JAIN CHIEF (*again mockingly*): Oh, then, your god is just an ordinary human being?

RAMANUJAR: Yes. Our God is born as a human being and subjects Himself to all human emotions like love and frustration, pleasure and sorrow. That is why man is able to merge himself with the Divine. That is what we call *Sowlabhyam*. Narayanan is easy of access. You could see him as the Rama who is separated from his wife and who sobs over her loss, you could see him as the Krishna who stole butter and who let Himself be punished for it by being tied to a stone mortar. Neela Devi listened to the music of Krishna's flute. The very joy of that music drove her affliction away.

JAIN CHIEF (*angrily*): You have deceived her playing some conjuror's trick.

RAMANUJAR: The magic trick is only this. It lies in realizing that we all belong to Narayanan, that we live only as we are in communion with Him, that we have no existence apart from Him. That is indeed the magic trick. And if the one who accepts responsibility is Narayanan Himself, what can we not achieve?

BITTALADEVAN: Swami, you still have not responded to our entreaty.

RAMANUJAR: What entreaty?

BITTALADEVAN: Please ask for whatever you want and we shall give it.

RAMANUJAR: Call all the people of your country and provide a feast to them. That is all I ask for.

JAIN CHIEF: We cannot partake of the feast.

RAMANUJAR: Why not?

BITTALADEVAN: I am one with a deformity. I have a finger missing. The Jain ascetics won't take part in a feast hosted by me.

RAMANUJAR: Mahaveera was the one who fought against superstitions of Brahminical religion. What new foolish belief is this, O chief of Jains?

JAIN CHIEF: This is our belief. You have no right to interfere.

RAMANUJAR: In the Vaishnavite religion there is room for everyone. Brahmins, Panchamas, the deformed—all are God's creation. Please arrange for the feast. We will all take part.

JAIN CHIEF: The king cannot do anything in violation of our religious decree.

BITTALADEVAN: I will. Tomorrow is the feast.

JAIN CHIEF (*furious*): We will excommunicate you from our religion.

BITTALADEVAN: Do. I will be only too happy. I am a Vaishnavite from today. Oh Ramanujar, bless me.

(*Exit the Jain chief in rage. Bittaladevan and Chandala Devi rise, go to Ramanujar, and prostrate themselves before him. He blesses them.*)

RAMANUJAR: From today your name will be Vishnu Vardhana Rayar. Om Namo Narayanaya.

(*Darkness.*)

SCENE 8

(*Darkness, as the curtain rises. After a few seconds, enter six men with torches. They go through the motions of clearing the thick growth of the forest with a sickle and thus slowly moving forward.*)

MAN 1: This is a real forest if ever there was one.

MAN 2: Snake holes ...

MAN 3: *Tulasi*[89] plants ...

MAN 4: Scary-looking mushrooms ...

MAN 5: The sun himself dare not enter here ...

MAN 6: Our job is to clear the forest here. It is Udaiyavar's order. We will carry it out.

MAN 1: We will give up even our life for the sake of Udaiyavar who has given us Panchamas a home and a life.

MAN 2: Udaiyavar says that if we clear this forest we will find Narayanan. Is that true?

MAN 3: Nothing he says will prove false.

MAN 4: What is this forest called?

MAN 5: Yadugiri forest.

MAN 5: It is Udaiyavar's surmise that we will also find *tiruman*[90], the symbol of Vaishnavism, here.

(*While these exchanges are going on, Man 1 has been looking down at the earth intently. His face fills with wonder as he bends, picks up something and holds it near the torch to see what it is. Men 2, 3, 4, 5, and 6 look at him.*)

MAN 1: A gold ornament!

(*The others move close to him and look at what he has in his hand.*)

OTHERS (*in wonder*): Yes, it is an ornament.

(*Enter at this point Ramanujar, also with a torch and a sickle in his hands. The men delightedly approach him and hand the 'ornament' to him.*)

MAN 1: This was found here.

(Ramanujar studies 'it' carefully for a few seconds.)

RAMANUJAR (*delighted*): Yes, it is the Lord's ornament. Yes, most certainly Narayanan will be here too. (*He joins them in the work.*)
RAMANUJAR: We will feel no fatigue if we sing as we work. Shall we sing?

(*The rhythmic beat of cymbals is heard in the background as he sings.*)

Pasuram

The discus grew, the conch and the bow also grew, the Earth resounded 'Hail!', the mace and the sword grew. The world became a bubble, the Lord's foot touched the Asura's head. Oh! How my father grew and strode the Earth, heralding a new age!

What sounds arose when my father churned for ambrosia! The rivers lashed water backwards over mountains, the ocean swirled in waves back and forth, as a snake-wrapped mountain grated the Earth.

The seven plains stood firmly in place, the seven mountains stood firmly in place, the seven oceans stood firmly in place, when my father lifted the Earth with his tusk teeth![91]

(*At this point, Man 4, who has been working at C, shouts in joy. The music stops.*)

MAN 4: *Ayya*, ... please come and see what we have here.

(*Ramanujar moves quickly to that spot. He bends to see what lies there.*)

RAMANUJAR: We sang, '... full of nectar'. We have found nectar itself. This is indeed the *moolavar* idol.

(*He prostrates himself before it. So do the others.*)

RAMANUJAR (*to the men*): They are sinners who call you Panchamas ... You should properly be called *Tirukkulattar*,[92] the people who belong to the noble caste—the people who found tiruman. Our Father in his avatar as *Varaha*[93] found the earth, which had been hidden under the sea, and brought it up holding it between his teeth. And now your sickle has found the hidden *Hari* and given Him back to the world. O Tirukkulattar, you are an avatar too. My obeisance to you!

(*He falls prostrate before them. Taken aback by this unexpected gesture, they, however, stop him.*)

RAMANUJAR: Let *Melukote* henceforth be known as *Tirunarayanapuram*. We will speak to King Vishnuvardhanan and raise a temple here. And you will always have the first honours in this temple.

(*He pauses for a while as though he had suddenly thought of something.*)

MAN 2: What are you thinking about, Ayya?

RAMANUJAR: We will build a temple and perform the consecration ceremony for it, but ...

MAN 2: But ...

RAMANUJAR: We have found the moolavar idol. But we need the *utsavar* idol too, don't we? All right. ... We will search for it tomorrow. This will do for today.

(*Exeunt all. Darkness.*

When the lights come on again, we see Ramanujar standing beside Vishnuvardhanan at C. Vishnuvardhanan's countenance is radiant. He appears to have communicated something to Ramanujar just now. It is morning.)

RAMANUJAR: Who is the 'enemy king' you speak of?

VISHNUVARDHANAN: It is the Turkish king. When he invaded this land, his men took away a lot of things from here. People say that this utsava idol, which is one of the things they took away, is now with his daughter.

RAMANUJAR: With his daughter?

VISHNUVARDHANAN: It seems she plays with it as with a doll.

RAMANUJAR: No wonder. Whatever one takes Narayanan to be, He becomes that. ... I have an idea.

VISHNUVARDHANAN: Please tell us what it is.

RAMANUJAR: I will go see that king and ...

VISHNUVARDHANAN (*shocked*): What are you saying? You go and see a Turkish king?

RAMANUJAR: Why not? He is a human being, after all. I am sure I can talk to him as one human being to another.

VISHNUVARDHANAN: But if some harm befalls you ...

RAMANUJAR: Nothing will happen. Ranganathan will take care. In fact I could have gone and talked to the Chola king too earlier. Somehow it didn't strike me then. However, I realize only now that Ranga had other duties for me to carry out then. I will now see this Muslim king taking with me my Tirukkulattar.

(*Exit Ramanujar. The king stands still in a shocked state. Darkness.*)

SCENE 9

(*When the lights return, we see a throne with a large green curtain behind it. The Turkish king is seated on the throne. He appears quite young, well below 30. In front of him are the courtiers, occupying decorated seats.*

A few seconds after the lights come on, a soldier enters from L end of the forestage and performs a salaam *to the court.*)

COURTIER 1(*to the soldier*): What is the matter?

SOLDIER: There is someone to see His Majesty.

KING: Bring him.

(*Enter Ramanujar and two men of the Tirukkulam. They perform a salaam before the King. It must be a new experience for the Muslim king to receive a salaam from a Hindu ascetic. He raises his eyebrows in surprise, and looks at Ramanujar.*)

KING: Who are you?

RAMANUJAR: My name is Ramanujar. I am a Vaishnavite.

KING: What does 'Vaishnavite' mean?

RAMANUJAR: Vaishnavites are those who believe that all things in the world have meaning only in relation to God.

KING (*mocking*): God! But aren't there many gods in your religion?

RAMANUJAR: There is only one God. He may be Allah, He may be Narayanan. It is only the names that are different. There is only one God.

KING: What? ... Na ... ra ... yanan?

RAMANUJAR: It is a logically appropriate name.[94] He is in all things. He is all things, all states, subtle and gross.

KING: Does God have form?

RAMANUJAR: For that matter, God has no name either. However, in order to explain Him to ourselves, don't we give Him a name and call Him Allah? Form is also like that. If someone firmly believes that a particular form is God, then that form is indeed God for him.

KING: A clever answer. And which is the form that you believe in?

RAMANUJAR: It is inside the royal ladies' chamber.

KING (*taken aback*): What are you saying?

RAMANUJAR: People say that during your last invasion, a lot of things were brought here from the temple at Tondanur. One of them is the god I worship, an idol.

COURTIER (*rising*): The things brought here were things given to us as tribute. Such things are never returned.

(*The king motions to him to sit.*)

KING: Well, it was not I but my father who made the invasion. As for me, I hate wars altogether. Nor do I like looting other people's possessions. ... But, putting that aside, do you know for certain that this idol is with us?

RAMANUJAR: That is what I have heard. They said that a girl in your ladies' chamber is playing with it.

(*The king thinks for a while.*)

KING (*after a few seconds*): Yes, I understand. My younger sister has an idol in her possession. I have seen her playing with it. All right, please come ... we will go the ladies' chamber and ... (*Rises.*)

COURTIER 1 (*rising*): Your Majesty ...

KING (*over his shoulder*): What?

COURTIER 1: It is not proper to take a person of another land and another religion into the royal ladies' chamber.

KING (*with a smile*): This is an elderly man. An ascetic. Your taboos won't apply to him. Besides, restrictions are never to be enforced on good people. (*To Ramanujar*) Please come.

(*They exit through L end of the rear stage. The courtiers sit looking at one another. They clearly do not like what the king is doing. Darkness.*

When the lights come on after a few seconds, the green curtain remains but the seats have been removed.

Sitting in kneeling position at C is a Muslim girl, about 8 years old. She is talking to the idol in front of her. She is very pretty and dressed in accordance with Islamic custom. Ramanujar and the king, who enter through R end of the rear stage, stand silently behind her and listen. There is soft light falling soothingly on the eyes.)

GIRL: How lovely you look! (*She takes up the idol, hugs it to her heart, kisses it, and then puts it back.*) I will never leave you. I will always play only with you. You are my treasure. (*She picks up the idol, kisses it, and puts it back.*) The *mullah*[95] says that you are the god of the *kafirs*.[96] Isn't there only one God? That is what the Koran says, the mullah tells me. If that is true, how can there be one God for the kafirs and another for the believers? But you are not my God, you are my lord and bridegroom. (*The king, a little taken back at this, looks at Ramanujar. There is a smile on Ramanujar's face.*) You must remain with me forever. I will never leave you. How lovely you are! No, I will never part with you.

KING (*smiling*): The time for parting has indeed come, my dear sister.

(*Startled, the girl rises and looks at them. She sees Ramanujar and looks at him in wide-eyed perplexity and quickly picks up and hides the idol behind her back.*)

KING: That idol belongs to this person. Give it to him, Raziya.

GIRL (*obstinately*): No, it is mine.

RAMANUJAR (*smiling*): It belongs to both of us.

RAZIYA: No. It belongs only to me. He is the one I am going to marry.

KING (*smiling*): Well, you will be the only Muslim girl to marry a Hindu god, Raziya.

RAMANUJAR: Most certainly. (*Pointing to the idol.*) He will have no objection to that. Whatever state anyone wants to see Him in, He will not hesitate to enter that state. We can regard him as anything whatsoever—as husband, father, son. I now regard Him as my darling child.

KING (*smiling*): In that case, you should give him in marriage to this girl.

RAMANUJAR: Well, that is what one of our ancestors did. But what he did was to give his daughter in marriage to this Lord. As he became father-in-law to the Divine Himself, he was known as *Periyazhwar,* Elder Azhwar.[97]

RAZIYA: What was the name of that girl?

RAMANUJAR: Andal.

RAZIYA: I too am his wife, like Andal.

KING: All right, enough of this sport. Hand this idol to him.

RAZIYA: No, I won't.

KING: He has to return to his place.

RAZIYA: Let him. But I won't part with this. I will be with him forever.

(*The king, at a loss, looks at Ramanujar.*)

RAMANUJAR: This idol has to be installed at the temple at Melukote. After that, ...

RAZIYA: In that case, I will go with you. Aren't you my father-in-law?

(*Ramanujar looks at the king. The king stands silent.*)

RAMANUJAR: We have no right to stand in the way of this profound affection of the soul.

KING: So ...?

RAMANUJAR: I will take Raziya with me. I will bring her up like my own daughter. Have no fear, Your Majesty.

(*The king ponders this.*)

RAZIYA (*pleading, holding the king's hands*): Let me, let me go with him. Grant me permission, Elder Brother.

KING: All right, you go in. I need to talk to him.

(*She leaves.*)

KING: This girl is the daughter of my father's third wife. I can't now say what might have happened to her if I had not been around. I feel I can trust you. All right, take her with you. But you should not attempt to convert her from her religion. That promise I want from you.

RAMANUJAR: I vow to you in the name of the God I worship. I will not change her religion. She will be known from now and forever as *Turukka Nachiyar*.[98] And, there will be a shrine for her in all our temples, as there is one for our Andal. It is certain that people ages hence will keep talking of this divine Vaishnavite–Muslim connection.

(*The king gratefully holds Ramanujar's hands. Darkness.*)

Scene 10

(*It is a festive setting as the lights come on. It is morning. The Tirukkulattar are dancing with all bustle and energy to the beat of drums. Standing behind them rear stage and enjoying the dance are Ramanujar, Kidambi Achan, Mudaliyandan, the disciples, and Vishnuvardhanan. The dance and the drum beat rise in a crescendo.*

At this point, enter, from behind the audience opposite the stage, some more Tirukkulattar, holding the utsava idol, Chellappillai, with Raziya keeping close to the deity. The blowing of a conch is heard.

The shouting of 'Om Namo Narayanaya' resounds in the air. As the utsava deity approaches the stage, Ramanujar, accompanied by the others, receives it with the chanting of mantras.

Four of the Tirukkulattar, who are carrying the utsavar idol on their shoulders, now reach C of rear stage and stand there. The Tiruppallandu pasuram, composed by Periyazhwar, is now sung.)

Pasuram

May You have many years, many years, many thousands of years and many crores of thousands of years more. O gem-hued Lord with mighty wrestling shoulders, your red lotus feet are our refuge for ever and ever.[99]

(*When the singing is over, Mudaliyandan performs the camphor arti[100] to the deity. Kidambi Achan distributes holy water to everyone and places the* satari[101] *on everyone's head. When the ceremony is over, Ramanujar moves and stands at C of stage.*)

RAMANUJAR: To those who believe in Narayanan Nambi everything that happens is according to His will. Alavandar's ambition was the reign of Narayanan in all lands. Today is indeed the golden day on which our gurunathar's dream has come true. Let us express our gratitude to the Chola king too on this occasion. This Tirunarayanapuram, also known as Melukote, will henceforth be a sacred shrine for all Vaishnavites. The Turukka Nachiyar, who gave us our *Sampatkumaran*, is mother to all of us from now.

(*He walks to Raziya and embraces her. There is then the chanting of Om Namo Narayanaya. Silence for a while.*)

RAMANUJAR: My task here is over and I must return to Srirangam. The *Fifty-two Men*[102] will remain and continue the Vaishnavite mission. Please give me leave to go. ...

(*There is a murmur among the rest. It is clear they don't want him to leave.*)

RAMANUJAR: I know you would not like me to leave. But ... I can't refuse Ranganathan's call. I can't go on without seeing Kuresar who has borne the scars of sacrifice on my account. Let me express my gratitude to King Vishnuvardhanan. And to you all. The prospering of Vaishnavism is now your responsibility. And you will always have the blessings of my Chellapillai.[103] Trust in him.

(*He takes leave of them and exits through L end of the forestage. Leaving with him are Kidambi Achan, Mudaliyandan, and disciples.*
The chanting of Om Namo Narayanaya is heard. Darkness.)

ACT IV

(When the lights come on, Ramanujar is seated at C of the rear stage. Near him on the two sides are Kidambi Achan, Mudaliyandan, Govinda Perumal (Embar), and disciples. It is morning. A pasuram is heard in the background.)

Pasuram

Behold, the lotus has bloomed in profusion, the sun has risen from the sea. Slender-waisted women with curly locks step out of the river onto the river bank, squeezing their hair dry and putting on their clothes. O Lord Ranga, surrounded by the surging waters of the Kaveri, bless this lowly serf, Tondarippodi, bearer of the flower basket, that he may serve your devotees. O Lord, arise![104]

(Ramanujar is rapt in the song.)

RAMANUJAR *(after the singing is over)*: At Tirunarayanapuram too this pasuram, so graciously composed and left for us by Tondaradippodi Azhwar, used to ring in my ears. And whenever it was heard, Ranganathan would appear before my very eyes.

(Silence. He seems to be thinking about something.)

RAMANUJAR: Why has Kuresar not yet come?

DISCIPLE 1: He is on his way, Swami.

RAMANUJAR: All my gurus have reached Tirunadu. Tirukkoshtiyur Nambi, Tirumalai Andan, the araiyar of the Srirangam temple, Tirukkachi Nambi, Periya Nambi. I know not what mission is left for me to perform yet; only Rangan knows.

(Enter now from L end of the forestage, the blind Kuresar, being led by his sons, Parasara Pattar and Sriramappillai (Vyaasa Pattar). Parasarar and Sriramappillai are both young men. Ramanujar rises from his seat, goes to Kuresar and embraces him. He then looks keenly at Parasarar and Sriramappillai for a few seconds.)

PARASARAR: I am Parasarar, he is my younger brother, Sriramappillai.

(*Ramanujar embraces them too one by one.*)

RAMANUJAR (*with intense feeling*): Oh Kuresar, what a terrible thing you did!

(*Kuresar smiles. Ramanujar leads them along and seats them near his own seat.*)

RAMANUJAR: What a sacrifice! There cannot be anything at all like this.

KURESAR: Swami, what are you saying? Where is the sacrifice?

RAMANUJAR: Shouldn't I have gone through all this in your place?

KURESAR (*smiling*): What I did was simply service to Vaishnavism. I did it with full awareness of what I was doing. Is it right for Udaiyavar, of all persons, to misinterpret it and call it sacrifice?

RAMANUJAR: Forgive me, I did not mean that you did it with a view to winning recognition as a martyr. From my point of view, it was a great sacrifice. After all, it was I who should have lost my eyes. Maybe, it is my sense of guilt …

KURESAR (*a little taken aback*): Your sense of guilt?

RAMANUJAR: Yes, the guilt that has been troubling me ever since I sent my gurunathar Periya Nambi and you to endure all this pain and sorrow and went away myself …

KURESAR: But if you hadn't gone away like that then, would Tirunarayanapuram ever have taken shape? Would we have got back Sampatkumaran?

RAMANUJAR: Well, come to think of it, that is the way we comfort ourselves trying to rationalize our acts of the past. All the same, my going away was indeed wrong.

KURESAR (*smiling*): Swami, I can't think of this as a great loss or privation. Well, I can't see the world. That's all. But I see Rangan all the time with my inner eye, without the interference of the external sights and scenes. What else do I want?

RAMANUJAR: Those external sights and scenes are also Rangan, O Kuresar. A true Vaishnavite needs both—an outer as well as an inner existence. You must see us all. Here are Kidambi Achan, Mudaliyandan, indeed all of us, waiting to be blessed by your *kataksha*[105] … Therefore … (*He pauses.*)

KURESAR: Therefore …? Please go on, Swami.

RAMANUJAR: We shall go to Kanchipuram and pray to Lord Varadan to restore your eyesight.

(*Kuresar laughs gently.*)

RAMANUJAR: Why do you laugh?

KURESAR (*smiling*): When you are quite visible to my inner eye, what need do I have of physical eyes? And there is a big advantage in seeing people with the inner eye. You then have the right to decide who you will see and who you will not.

RAMANUJAR: But there is nothing in the world that we should spurn as not worthy of sight. We can find nectar in poison, if Narayanan wills it. Please, for our sake, ... let us go to Kanchipuram and ...

KURESAR: There is no need to go to Kanchi. I can see Lord Varadan even in Rangan's shrine.

RAMANUJAR: If that is so, let us go today itself, right now, to Rangan's shrine. Come, let us start.

(*He rises, holds Kuresar's hand, and leads him away. The others follow. Darkness.*

When the lights come on, they are all standing in two rows, facing the audience. Ramanujar and Kuresar are at C. In front of them is the Lord's sanctum. The temple bell rings. When it stops, Kuresar begins to sing.)

Pasuram

O Lord of Mallai on the shores of the sea that washes ashore heaps of gems! O Lord of Kanchi surrounded by high walls! O Lord of Perunagar! The lord Siva who is spouse of Parvati—daughter of the mountain king Malaya—stands beside you. O Lord, reclining on the ocean of milk, O Lord of the Earth, O Lord, standing on snow-clad peaks! Where do you dwell? Wretch that I am, I wander piteously searching for you.[106]

(*Once again, the temple bell and the blowing of a conch. Silence for a few seconds after they stop. A voice is heard.*)

VOICE: You shed tears of musical joy and saw Varadan in Me. What boon shall I give you? Ask and it shall be granted unto you.

KURESAR: The grace that befalls me should be granted to Naluran too.

VOICE: So be it!

(*Everyone is shocked at this but not Ramanujar, who looks quietly at Kuresar for a few seconds and then smiles.*)

DISCIPLE 1 (*moving close to* KURESAR): Should that evil-doer be blessed with the same grace as you?

(*There is just a smile on Kuresar's face.*)

DISCIPLE 2: Why did you ask for such a boon?

KURESAR (*with a smile*): We can find nectar even in poison—with Narayanan's grace.

(*Ramanujar prostrates himself before Kuresar. It looks as though Kuresar senses this but does nothing to stop him. The others are shocked.*)

RAMANUJAR: Kuresar now stands in that blessed state which is beyond the petty existence susceptible to things such as friendship and enmity. The state he dwells in now is the ultimate ideal of Vaishnavism. Do you remember what Guhan said in the Ramayana? 'A thousand Ramas cannot equal one Bharata'?[107] In the same way, a thousand Ramanujars cannot equal one Kuresar. O, Kuresar, I pay you obeisance.

(*He once again prostrates himself before Kuresar. That Kuresar doesn't stop him is a little surprising to the others.*)

RAMANUJAR: Alavandar's three unfulfilled wishes ... a casteless society, salvation for the lowly ... that has now been realized at Tirunarayanapuram. At Srirangam? (*He heaves a big sigh.*) The second wish ... the narrow, insular, Vaishnava dharma should expand and enlarge beyond all limits. That too has been fulfilled. Under Chellappillai's sovereign sway, Melukote will prosper. The third wish ... an interpretation of the Brahmasutra in accordance with Visishtadvaita. It was granted to me to write that with the help of Kuresar and Andal Amma.

(*At this point Ramanujar calls Parasaran to his side. Parasaran goes.*)

RAMANUJAR: Here is Parasaran, the wonderful treasure that Kuresar has bequeathed to us. Here is a young man born to a rich tradition of holiness. He is Vaishnavism's most prized possession, our future, my heir.

(*The shy Parasaran shows his embarrassment at Ramanujar's pronouncement, which, however, throws all the others into joy. The temple bell and the blowing of a conch are heard.*)

RAMANUJAR: The Vaishnavite never dies. He has no beginning, no end. I am confident that Parasaran will complete the tasks that I have left unfinished. If we are blessed with divine grace, all that we see with our eyes is Vaikuntam. God is simply the ultimate bourne of all human possibilities. Let us continue our journey towards that goal. The journey has no end. Om Namo Narayanaya.

(*The cry of Om Namo Narayanaya resounds in the air. The temple bell rings, a conch is blown. Darkness.*)

NOTES AND GLOSSARY

1. Pasuram, meaning 'song', is specifically used in Tamil to refer to the hymns sung by the Azhwars in praise of Lord Vishnu. The pasurams sung by the twelve Azhwars, spread over 300 years (from late 6th to end 9th century AD), were collected by Nathamunigal (AD 910–90) into what is known as *Nalayira Divya Prabandham* (Four Thousand Sacred Verses).

2. Poygai Azhwar, *Vaiyam takaliya*, pasuram No. 2082 in *Nalayira Divya Prabandham*. The translations of all the pasurams included in the present play have been taken from *The Sacred Book of Four Thousand*, a translation of the *Nalayira Divya Prabandham* done by Srirama Bharati (Selvamudaiyanpettai Araiyar 2000). Hereafter the notes for the pasurams will be given in the following order: 1. Name of the Azhwar; 2. First words of the pasuram transliterated into English; and 3. *NDP* (standing for *Nalayira Divya Prabandham*), followed by the number of the pasuram in the collection.

3. Bootam, *Anbetakaliya*, NDP 2182.

4. Pey, *Tirukkanden*, NDP 2282.

5. See Supra, '*Life of Ramanujar*', p. xvii.

6. The Tamil way of referring to the Vaishnavite temple town of Srirangam.

7. Tondaradippodi, *Kadimalarkkamalangal*, NDP 926.

8. Lord Varadaraja, the Vishnu deity at the Kanchipuram temple.

9. Nammazhwar, *Soozhvisumpanimuhil*, NDP 3755.

10. The suffixes *-an* and *-ar* are used with Tamil nouns to convey distinctions of age and respect. *-ar* indicates respect. *-an* is generally used by a man when referring to himself.

11. The Vaishnavite way of referring to the blessed abode of the dead.

12. Vaikuntam is the sacred abode of Lord Vishnu, a place and state that every Vaishnavite aspires to attain and dwell in after the death of the body. Of the 108 sacred places (*Divya Desangal*) that the Vaishnavite aspires to visit as a pilgrim, 106 are located on earth (in India), the 107th is the mythical Ocean of Milk (*Tirupparkadal*), and the 108th is Vaikuntam (also called *Sri Vaikuntam, Paramapadam,* or *Tirunadu*).

13. Tirumangai Azhwar, *Kallaar Madil Soozh*, NDP 1541.

14. Tirukkachi Nambi was also respectfully called Kanchi Purna. *Kkachi* or Tirukkachi is Kanchi or Kanchipuram.

15. A respectful form of referring to (or addressing) the *guru* or teacher. Note also the third person form being used as direct address. This is again quite common as a marker of respect, especially in earlier forms of Tamil.

16. The Tamil Sri Vaishnavite term for food offering. See also 'The Point of View of the Epigrapher', pp. xxxiii and xxxiv'.

17. Saturdays in *Purattasi* (the sixth month in the Tamil calendar, roughly mid-September to mid-October) are regarded as particularly sacred to Vishnu and are marked by special observances with ritual purity.

18. The pial (called *tinnai* in Tamil) was a raised platform in front of a typical South Indian house of the past, usually before the main entrance. For the cultural significance of the space here, see 'Commentary on the Play'.

19. 'Prayer offered to the guest'. See also 'Commentary on the Play'.

20. Perumal is the Tamil Vaishnavite term for God or the deity.

21. Lord Krishna, Balarama, and Sudhama (Kuchela), were disciples of Sage Santipini. Periya Nambi means that Santipini must have been Krishna's guru only in a formal sense since Krishna was God Himself.

22. Acharam, a frequently used word in Brahmin parlance, can be translated as 'strict observance of orthodox principles and practices' or 'strict observance of the code'.

23. Tridandam (staff) and pavitram (pennant) are objects constantly carried by a Hindu monk. See also 'Commentary on the Play'.

24. Tondaradippodi, *Pacchai maamalaipol, NDP* 873.

25. Disciple.

26. Kulasekhara, *Muzhudum venney, NDP* 715.

27. Death anniversary ceremony. See 'Commentary on the Play' for more on this episode.

28. See 'Life of Ramanuja in History and Legend'.

29. *Ubhaya Vedantin*, in Vaishnavite parlance, is one who has mastered all the religious scriptures, including the Vedas and Tamil hymnal literature.

30. The word with eight sounds: *Om Namo Narayanaya*.

31. A polite way of addressing a stranger, especially a Brahmin.

32. The meaning of the sacred mantras.

33. *Vyasasutra* is another name for *Brahmasutra*. Every preceptor of Hindu religion wrote a commentary (or *Bhashya*) on Vyasa's *Brahmasutra*, the Upanishands, and the Bhagavad Gita. Ramanuja's commentary is hailed as *Sri Bhashyam*. He aimed at showing that *Brahmasutra* did not expound a principle of Ultimate Reality which is contentless and devoid of qualities. He attempted to interpret the text from the Visishtadvaita point of view in his *Sri Bhashyam*. He was aided in this task by the astute disciple Kuresa.

34. See 'Commentary on the Play'.

35. Motto, watchword.

36. Nammazhwar, *Poliga, poliga*. *NDP* 3128.

37. 'Our Lord.'

38. The insulting reference here is to the fact that Ramanujar came from Kanchipuram in northern Tamil Nadu to assume leadership of the Vaishnavite mutt based in Srirangam in southern Tamil Nadu. For more on the north–south divide, see A Critique of the Play *Ramanujar* in 'Hagiography Revisited'.

39. A Smartha is one who worships Siva and is generally construed as synonymous with Advaitin. A Vaishnavite is one who worships Vishnu. The relationship between the two sects is traditionally regarded as oppositional, if not adversarial.

40. The Chetti, Vaisya, or merchant caste.

41. Food offered to the deity and distributed among the devotees.

42. The holy water offered to the deity is distributed among the devotees in spoonfuls. The person among the devotees to whom it is given first should be a man of the highest caste, usually one of the temple priests. It is thus the height of sacrilege, according to the Brahmins here, to offer it first to a man from the cheri or slum, that is an untouchable.

43. The name Vyasa or Veda Vyasa is applied to Krishna Dvaipayana, the son of Sage Parasara and Satyavati, a fisherwoman. Vyasa (whose name literally means 'the arranger') is believed to have arranged or compiled the Vedas, the Puranas, and also the Mahabharata.

44. According to legend, Valmiki, the author of the *Ramayana*, was a hunter/bandit before he became a bard.

45. Tiruppaanzhwar (8th century AD). See 'Commentary on the Play'.

46. Another name for Tiruppanaazhwar.

47. Title conferred on Ramanuja.

48. Nammazhwar, *Poliga, poliga*. *NDP* 3128. *Poothangal* , which can mean 'spirits', has here been translated as 'apostles' in view of the context.

49. Female disciple.

50. Brahmin quarters.

51. Idol or image of the presiding deity in a temple taken out in procession in the streets during festivals for public worship. Cf. *moolavar* or the *moolavamurti* which means the main stationary idol in the shrine.

52. Wind instrument with long pipe, played in the temple or outside, during festivals.

53. Nammazhwar, *Payilum sudar oli*. *NDP* 2963.

54. Panchamas are the lowest in the Hindu social order, belonging to the fifth caste, the other four being Brahmana, Kshatriya, Vaisya, and Sudra.

55. A chieftain of the region under the Chola king who became Ramanuja's disciple and whom he later appointed the Superintendent of the Srirangam temple.

56. Andal, *Undu madakalittran*. NDP 491.

57. A view or glimpse. The word is used in Indian languages in relation to worship of a deity in a temple.

58. The discus Lord Vishnu holds in His right hand.

59. Tiruppanaazhwar, *Kondal vannanai*. NDP 936.

60. 'One who embodies in himself the beauty of the entire universe'. See Author's Preface and Commentary on Act I, Scene 7.

61. One who belongs to the warrior caste.

62. See Critique of the Play *Ramanujar*.

63. *Veshti* is a piece of cloth (measuring four or eight cubits) worn by Indian men around the waist and down the ankle.

64. Tondaradippodi, Amaravongamaarum. *NDP* 914. The reference is to the four Vedas (*Rig, Yajur, Saama and Atharva*) and the six *angas* or parts of the Vedas (called *Seeksha, Vyakarnam, Chhandas, Nrittam, Jyotisham, and Kalpam*).

65. Tirumangai, *Vaanavartangal*. NDP 1048. *Venkatam* (as well as *Tiruvenkatam*) stands for Tirupati. *Akhil* is eagle-wood.

66. *Parivattam* is a formal term referring to the piece of cloth wound round the head especially by holy men. Nowadays, it is used to refer to the piece of silk cloth which is first placed on the consecrated idol and then tied round the head of a distinguished person as a mark of blessing and honour.

67. Term of contempt for a Brahmin.

68. *Sridevi*, another name for Lakshmi, is the goddess of good fortune, wealth, and prosperity. Her elder sister, called *Moodevi*, is believed to bring misfortune.

69. After the attempt by the priests to poison Ramanuja, Tirukkottiyur Nambi nominated Kidambi Achan the acharya's cook (See GPP: 202).

70. Scriptures or treatises of Hindu religion.

71. 'No, it isn't': the famous Upanishadic utterance in Sanskrit, '*Neti, Neti*', which denies the reality of everything other than the Brahman. See 'Commentary on the Play.'

72. 'Attributeless God'.

73. See 'Commentary on the Play.'

74. The sacred thread (called *yagnopaveetam* in Sanskrit and *poonool* in Tamil) is worn across the chest by Brahmin males. Making Panchamas (men of the fifth, untouchable, caste) wear the sacred thread amounts to giving them a status equal to that of Brahmins.

75. *Tiruvaiymozhi*, comprising 1102 pasurams composed by Nammazhwar, is regarded as constituting the fourth thousand in the *Nalayira Divya*

Prabandham (Four Thousand Sacred Hymns). The other collections of pasurams sung by Nammazhwar, viz. *Tiruviruttam* (100 pasurams), *Tiruvasiriyam* (7), and *Periya Tiruvandadi* (87) are included in the third thousand.

76. The Srirangam Temple is known among Vaishnavites as the Big Temple (*Periya Koyil*).

77. Sacred ash (called *Tiruneeru* or *Vibhuti*) is worn on the forehead by Saivites.

78. 'Obeisance to Lord Siva!'

79. Panchaksharam is the five-lettered name of Lord Siva (*Na-ma-si-va-ya*).

80. The name of Lord Narayana (*Om Namo Narayanaya*).

81. See Life of Ramanuja in Legend and History in 'Hagiography Revisited'.

82. *Oorukkup pollaan, enakku nallaan* (Tamil). See ibid.

83. A place a few kilometres from Srirangam.

84. For Nathamuni, see 'The Place of Ramanujar in Indian Thought', p. xxxv and commentary on Act I, Scene 1. Kuruhai Kavalappan was a direct disciple of Nathamuni. He was taught Yoga by Nathamuni himself. Alavander was to learn it from Kuruhai Kavalappan, but he missed the appointment and went to Kerala to have darshan of the deity Sri Anantapadmanabha Swamy. This is considered to be an important turning point for Vaishnavism as it came to set the worship of deity above personal absorption in Yoga.

85. Prapatti is total surrender to the Lord which is the doctrine that the later southern Vaishnava sub-sect (*Tengalai*) came to emphasize.

86. Gokulam is the place where Lord Krishna spent his days as a boy in the midst of cowherds and dairy maids. Hence Gokulam became synonymous in the Hindu mind with innocence and joyful community.

87. Brindavan is a place now in the north Indian state of Uttar Pradesh. In Purana literature, it is the blissful place near Gokulam where Krishna spent his youth.

88. Periayzhwar, *Siruviralhal tadavi*. NDP 282.

89. Basil plant, sacred to Lord Krishna.

90. See Life of Ramanuja in Legend and History in 'Hagiography Revisited'.

91. Namazhwar, *Aazhiezha, aaru malaikku* and *naanrila vezh*. NDP 3370–2.

92. See Life of Ramanuja in Legend and History in 'Hagiography Revisited' and 'Commentary on the Play'.

93. Lord Vishnu took the form of a boar and lifted the earth on his tusk and saved it from inundation.

94. *Narayana* is etymologically one who dwells in (and one in whom dwell) all things (*nara*), living and non-living.

95. Muslim teacher of religion and holy law.

96. Non-Muslim (usually derogatory).

97. Periyazhwar (ninth century AD) was a devotee of Lord Vishnu and made garlands for the temple deity at Srivilliputtur (in south Tamil Nadu) daily. He found a baby girl abandoned in the garden and brought her up naming her Andal. One day, without her father's knowledge, Andal put on the garland meant for the Lord because of her passionate love for Him. She continued to do this for many days before her foster father saw her wearing the garland and chided her for it. But the Lord appeared in Periyazhwar's dream and told him how happy He was to wear the garland first worn by his devotee. At the Lord's command, conveyed through the temple priest, Periyazhwar took his daughter to the sanctum in the Srirangam temple to give her in marriage to the Lord Himself. According to legend, Andal, standing in front of Lord Ranganatha, sang hymns in His praise and merged with Him. She is worshipped as one of the twelve Azhwars and her compositions, *Tiruppavai* (comprising thirty pasurams) and *Nachiyar Tirumozhi* (143 pasurams) are included in the first thousand of the *Nalayira Divya Prabandham*.

98. Turukka is Tamil for 'Turk' and Nachiyar is the title given to the female saints in ancient Tamil country. See Life of Ramanuja in Legend and History in 'Hagiography Revisited' and 'Commentary on the Play'.

99. Periyazhwar, *Pallaandu, pallaandu*. NDP 1. This is the first pasuram in the *Nalayira Divya Prabandham* and is sung in Vishnu temples and orthodox Vaishnavite households as part of the daily prayer.

100. Arti is the ceremonial whirling of burning camphor before the deity, a Hindu ritual in worship.

101. Satari is the small metallic object on which Vishnu's feet are engraved and which is placed over the head of a worshipper as a sign of blessing.

102. See 'The Point of view of the Epigrapher', p. xxxiv.

103. Chellapillai: literally, 'darling', the utsava (processional) idol in the Melukote temple.

104 Tondaradippodi, *Kadimalark kamalangal*. NDP 926.

105. Kataaksham is the Divine casting his eye of Benediction upon the devotee. Here Ramanujar means that Kuresar should regain his vision and bless the others by looking at them.

106. Tirumangai Azhwar, *Vangattal maamani*. NDP 2060.

107. In the Ramayana, Bharata coming to know of the banishment of his elder brother Rama by their father Dasaratha, travels to the forest across the river Ganges, to beg Rama to take back the kingdom. Guha, the chieftain of the boatmen who ferry Bharata across the river, speaks these words in praise and wonder.

COMMENTARY ON THE PLAY

PROLOGUE

The prologue sets the scene several centuries before Ramanuja by dramatizing a very famous legend about the three primal Azhwars in Tamil country known as Pei, Poigai, and Bhootam. The story involving these three Vaishnavite mystics is a well-known narrative in Vaishnavite lore, stressing the mystical experiences of these Azhwars on a stormy night in a place near Tirukkovilur. Each one of them has a vision of the Divine in utter darkness which transports them, into a transcendental experience. Each one bursts into a hymn that takes him in an upward movement to a moment of sublime self-realization. Indira Parthasarathy's purpose in beginning his play on Ramanuja with this episode seems to be twofold: i) The origins of Vaishnavism lie in the mystical experiences of the Azhwars of the supremacy of Lord Narayana; ii) humanism and empathy are the indisputable paths to the Divine. The playwright hence uses the hymns of the three Azhwars intertextually to reiterate that the acharyas (preceptors) of Vaishnavism, including Ramanuja, derive their humane spirituality from the tradition of the Azhwars. In this episode, thunder and rain press these mendicant mystics one after the other to a shelter, compelling each to think of the elemental needs of the other person rather than entertain selfish thoughts about comfort and security for oneself. Thus the hovel in which they are forced to huddle together becomes the site of manifestation of Divine light. Hence, in each hymn, the dominant image and image clusters have to do with the lamp, wick, ghee, light, and, finally, enlightenment and vision. Enlightenment comes only in a moment when one realizes, 'Thy need is greater than mine.' When such a realization dawns on the soul the Lord reveals Himself in all splendour. Hence the third song uses the phrase 'I have seen' in a reiterative manner. The Prologue thus serves the purpose of highlighting the humanist spiritual tradition from which Ramanuja descends. It also prepares the reader for a redefinition of the term 'Vaishnava' which occurs as a lietmotif throughout the play. The query—who is a Vaishnava?—is not to be answered simply as 'he who worships Vishnu'. A Vaishnava is one who cannot see another man suffer and this is the definition derived from the import of Nammazhwar's *Tiruvaymozhi*.

ACT I

SCENE 1

The play proper begins with one of the greatest Vaishnava acharyas, Yamunacharya known as Alavandar, in his last days when he is searching for a disciple who will carry the torch forward. Alavandar (perhaps born in AD 953 at Madurai) was the grandson of the great Nathamuni (b. AD 908) who was the first to conceive of Vaishnavism as a doctrine and who initiated a few disciples into this school of thought. J.B. Carman observes that 'Nathamuni was a Brahmin from a family with a tradition of Sanskrit scholarship'. He surmises, 'It may well have been one of the Brahmin families that had migrated from North India a few centuries before, under the inducement of land from the Hindu dynasty of the Pallavas' (1983:24). It is possible that the local Brahmin community benefited from the Sanskrit learning and prestige of Nathamuni's family and accepted its leadership when he was invited to move from his home Veeranarayanapuram, also known as Kattumannarkoil. Nathamuni's grandson was Yamuna who showed admirable erudition and intelligence in the court of a king in a philosophical debate with a well-known Pandit named Akki Azhwan. Because Yamuna defeated him with such consummate ease and brilliance, the queen hailed him as 'the one who has come to rule' (*Alavandar*). After taking over the throne from the king and ruling for sometime, Yamuna was called back to scriptural study and initiation into Yoga by his grandfather's disciple, Rama Mishra or Manakkal Nambi. Yamuna renounced secular powers to become the spiritual leader of the small Vaishnava community that had formed around Nathamuni. Alavandar is remembered not only for his scholarly doctrinal works such as *Siddhitraya* and *Stotraratna* (in Sanskrit), but also for the propagation of the Tamil hymns collectively called 'Four Thousand' or *Divya Prabandham*. Above all, he is hailed by legend for going beyond the orthodox caste distinctions of his times and inviting into his fold and cherishing a *Panchama* or outcaste devotee called Maraner Nambi. This spiritual egalitarianism of Alavandar is what is foregrounded in this scene. Alavandar is apparently in a state of introspection trying to articulate the quintessence of his doctrine of Vaishnavism. In the traditional legends called *Guruparampara* (the Line of Preceptors) it is said that when Ramanuja rushed to Srirangam to meet Alavandar to adopt him as his *guru*, Alavandar had just died and was about to be interred. Ramanuja saw that three of his fingers were folded and was curious to know what this meant. The disciples standing around thought that the folded fingers perhaps denoted his three wishes.[1]

Indira Parthasarathy, however, states in his Preface to the play that he deliberately gave an ideological underpinning to the first two wishes because in his opinion such a far-sighted acharya, who wanted to spread an enlightened doctrine, could not have conceived of naïve desires as having far-reaching consequences for the society. For example, the hagiography surrounding Alavandar mentions that he wanted to name Vaishnava children after sage Veda Vyasa and his father sage Parasara, and also after the greatest of the Azhwars, Nammazhwar. As a modern playwright with a revisionist sense of history, Indira Parthasarathy thinks that the first two wishes must be in consonance with the third wish. He finds it somewhat ridiculous to reduce the stature of Alavandar by interpreting his wishes so literally. Hence the first wish of Alavandar in this play is to uplift the outcaste and the oppressed and establish a casteless society. The second wish metamorphoses into a desire to see the expansion of an enlightened Vaishnavism. Thus Indira Parthasarathy alters the text and textuality of hagiographic writings along the lines of the thinking of Vaishnava acharyas. His justification for this rewriting is the fact that Alavandar was the progenitor of Ramanuja in social reform and that social reform is not separate from spiritual reform. Even traditional legends about Alavandar narrate how and in what situation he first encountered Maraner Nambi. The Panchama farmer was ploughing the land and when he felt hungry, because he was poor, he swallowed the slush in the field to appease his hunger. Alavandar, who witnessed this, was struck by the absolute spiritual realization of

[1] See *Life of Ramanuja* in History and Legend in 'Hagiography Revisited'.

Nambi on the nature of the body and the soul (Kalyanarama Iyengar 1978: 231). It is the playwright's contention that such a great preceptor would have wished for a profound ideal to be fulfilled. In the same scene we also note the redefinition of a Vaishnava. He is one who is beyond mortality and caste distinctions. This scene presents Ramanuja as proffering such a definition and conception of a Vaishnava at the funeral of Alavandar. He starts his spiritual career at this point, setting himself the goal of reaching the frontiers of possibilities.

SCENE 2

In this scene, the focus is on the dynamics of caste distinctions in Hindu society which Ramanuja tried to reform. We find Ramanuja searching for a preceptor after the death of Alavandar. Of the six prominent disciples of Alavandar, Kanchi Purna, known in Tamil as Tirukkachi Nambi, was performing the task of fanning Lord Varadaraja in the Kanchipuram temple. Ramanuja wants to prostrate himself before Tirukkachi Nambi and adopt him as his guru. Nambi, who accepts the code of conduct governing Hindu society, turns down this request of Ramanuja on the grounds of Hindu dharma. He is a 'Vaisya' (belonging to the merchant class which constitutes the third rung of Hindu society) who cannot receive such an honour from a Brahmin. The interesting feature here is the argument between Tirukkachi Nambi and Ramanuja on the efficacy of Karma. Nambi believes in Karma and its logical relation to caste. Even his total dedication to temple service does not entitle him to such an honour in his opinion. We can understand how Bhakti movement at this point of time had not effaced caste distinctions in reality, though it had brought into prominence men and women from the outcaste sections as well as the low castes. When Ramanuja contends that a Vaishnava is neither a Brahmin nor a Vaisya, Nambi points out that despite Alavandar's endeavours the caste system is still dominant. Ramanuja assures him that with his taking over the reins of Vaishnavism, the pride of caste will exist no more. The Tamil biographer Kalyanarama Iyengar points out that 'Tirukkachi Nambi's caste is now known as Bel Chettis' (Kalyanrama Iyengar 1978: 166).

An additional feature of the scene is the dramatization of how caste actually operates in society. Ramanuja invites Tirukkachi Nambi for a meal hoping to eat whatever is left over as a mark of respect to him. In the Tamil biographies there are two separate events that are collapsed here into one scene by Indira Parthasarathy. One takes place before Ramanuja's marriage when he meets Tirukkachi Nambi and offers to prostrate before him. The other takes place after his marriage to Tanjamma when he invites Tirukkachi Nambi for a meal. Tirukkachi Nambi hesitates to accept the invitation knowing well how a Brahmin housewife would treat a lower-caste person. His suspicions are proved true because Tanjamma, who hails from the Somayaji lineage (orthodox Vaidiki Brahmins), refuses to oblige. The scene deftly captures the disdain of a woman who is conscious of her social status expressed through her taunting of her husband for his lack of pride. Hers is the voice of rigid orthodox Brahminism in medieval Hindu society. Ramanuja as a man assumes that a wife follows the beliefs and values of her husband. But his spirit of egalitarianism is not shared by his wife.

SCENE 3

This scene captures the social reality in terms of people's attitudes and reactions. When Tirukkachi Nambi goes to Ramanuja's house in the latter's absence he accepts Tanjamma's hospitality on her terms. She asks him to be seated on the pial where she feeds him. From the point of view of caste, space is a very important trope which represents the ideological positions of the people. Here the pial signifies the social limits beyond which a person of lower caste cannot go. Ramanuja's wife's action of washing the place afterwards is not at all surprising given the Hindu social organization. As Carman remarks, 'Ramanuja's wife had the usual Brahmin attitude towards those of all lower castes and even toward other Brahmins of subcastes considered inferior to one's own. And this attitude is typically expressed as a fear of ritual pollution' (1974: 32). In fact, in the sources the act is described graphically. She uses a stick to remove the plantain leaf on which food was served to Tirukkachi Nambi and then cleans the place using cowdung mixed with water and begins to cook afresh after bathing again (GPP 6000: 167).

Tanjamma's use of the term *atithi puja* is ironic since she has indeed insulted the guest by serving him food on the *pial*. In fact, since

Ramanuja had called Tirukkachi Nambi his guru and said that the guru is to be regarded as one's father, she has violated all the three Upanishadic commands: *Pitru devo bhava, acharya devo bhava, atithi devo bhava* (Worship the father as God, worship the teacher as God, worship the guest as God).

The scene ends with an intertextual use of a verse from *Tirukkural* in which a guest is compared to an *aniccha* flower. Ramanuja uses this image to refer to Tirukkachi Nambi's sensitive being which Tanjamma has hurt by her acharam.

SCENE 4

This scene reiterates the basic humanism of Ramanuja as a householder (*grhasta*). As ever his wife is concerned more about superficial sanctity than about genuine human need. She would not feed a poor man who is hungry whereas Ramanuja is moved by his poverty. Parthasarathy follows the *Guruparampara* source fairly closely even in the style of the dialogue:

> One day a poor Sri Vaishnava [presumably non-Brahmin] came to oil massage Ramanuja. He looked weak and exhausted. Ramanuja called his wife and said, 'the poor Sri Vaishanava is hungry. Is there any left over food (*paryushithannam illayo*)'. She promptly replied, 'Not even a morsel'. Ramanuja sent her on some errand, went into the kitchen found some leftover food, called his wife and chided her, 'How can you do this, knowing well that a Sri Vaishnava is hungry?' (GPP 6000: 172)

SCENE 5

This scene shows the intensification of Ramanuja's disappointment with his married life. Parthasarathy follows the source narratives in presenting the quarrel between Ramanuja's wife and the wife of Maha Purna (Periya Nambi), one of the preceptors of Ramanuja. In the biographies, Ramanuja is said to have learnt one special text or set of doctrines each from five of Alavandar's chief disciples. Maha Purna is also the one who initiated Ramanuja at Madurantakam into the spiritual mode of life of a Sri Vaishnava. In this scene, he has come with his wife as Ramanuja's guest for six months. But the sense of social superiority that Ramanuja's wife betrays compels Periya Nambi and his wife to leave Ramanuja's house and go back to Srirangam. There is a sharp contrast between the disdain that Ramanuja's wife feels towards her guest and Ramanuja's own humility and his gratitude for all that he has learnt from Maha Purna, even as the all-knowing Lord Krishna learnt from the guru Sandipini. Here, Indira Parthasarathy echoes verbatim Ghoshti Purna in the sources but transfers the context from Maladhara (one of the five disciples of Alavandar mentioned in 'Life of Ramanuja') to Maha Purna (GPP 6000: 199). It is revealing that there is discrimination even within the Brahmin fold. It may seem ridiculous that Tanjamma should object to her pot being touched by Maha Purna's wife's pot. But Ramanuja's wife is conscious of her lineage and her husband's, which derives from the well-known Asuri family (an orthodox Vaidiki clan). There is a social dimension to the sense of superiority that Ramanuja's wife feels towards Maha Purna's wife. As Carman points out, Maha Purna belonged to a slightly lower sub-sect of 'forelock Brahmins', also called *brahacharanam* who wore their sacred tuft further forward on their heads and with whom the higher *vadama* sub-sect did not have marriage alliances (1974: 32). There is profound intertextual use by the playwright of an utterance from *Guruparamparai Prabhavam* (6000: 166) where Kanchi Purna expresses his gratitude to Lord Varadaraja saying, 'I who was substanceless have been made an entity' and thereby rejects Ramanuja's attributing any greatness or merit to him. Parthasarathy transfers this in the play to Ramanuja, who acknowledges his gratitude to Maha Purna for teaching him the scriptures. Thus the intertextuality serves to heighten the contrast between Ramanuja and his wife. Ramanuja is forced to take *sanyasa* because of his wife's incompatible outlook and values. The *Guruparampara* narrates it thus: 'Already you committed the sin of *Bhagavata apacharam* (insulting the Lord's devotees). Now you have picked up a quarrel with Periya Nambi's wife and committed *Asahyapachara* (insulting equals out of intolerance). You who behave like this, must leave' (GPP 6000: 173).

SCENE 6

Some of the sources say that Ramanuja asked his wife to go to her family for a wedding and in her absence he went to Lord Vardaraja's

sanctum and took the triple staff called *tridanda* to distinguish himself
from the *advaitins* who hold a single staff or *eka danda* and who also
cast off the sacred thread. He became 'Ramanuja Muni': 'He took
ochre robes and triple staff' (GPP 6000: 174). Parthasarathy puts his
stamp on the event by making Ramanuja declare that he is a social
being and hence he renounces family ties. Similarly there is a
redefinition of Vaishnavism. His vision of this new faith is
comprehensive and all encompassing, like Vishnu in his Vamana
Avatara who took two steps and measured the entire universe. All
such departures from the sources by the playwright serve to project
Ramanuja as an ideal human being.

SCENE 7

Ramanuja has established himself at Kanchipuram. Parthasarathy
compresses various events and episodes in Ramanuja's life into
dramatically significant scenes. Thus Act I foregrounds Ramanuja's
youth and his grhasta life after renouncing which he spends time as
an ascetic serving the Lord at the Kanchi temple. Eventually he
becomes the pontiff of the Srirangam *mutt*. This also entails a shift
from the northern town of Kanchipuram to the southern town of
Srirangam, which is in the heart of the Chola kingdom. He assumes
leadership of the developing Vaishnava community, attracting
intelligent and dedicated youngsters to the service of the new faith.
In the last scene of Act I we find out how Kuresa, the foremost and
most intelligent of his disciples, seeks him out. Parthasarathy, once
again, fuses the various episodes relating to Ramanuja's life between
Kanchipuram and Srirangam to bring focus to bear on his progressive
thinking and humane responses to the world. That is why in this scene
we find Ramanuja receiving his very first teacher Yadava Prakasa, who
is now much older, into his mutt as a disciple. This reversal of the
guru–sishya role is not uncommon in Ramanuja's life. In the sources,
Yadava Prakasa, who was a great advaitic teacher (of the *Bhedabheda*
school of Bhaskara) taught Ramanuja the Vedas and the Upanishads.
The most famous episode during this tutelage concerns Ramanuja
countering Sankara's interpretation of a verse from *Chandogya
Upanishad* (1.6.7) that compared the eyes of the Lord to the red
posteriors of a monkey (*'tasya yatha kapyasam pundarikameva*

makshini'). This hurt the young Ramanuja so deeply that he came out with a different etymological interpretation of the same verse: the eyes of the Lord are red as the lotus which blooms when the sun's rays touch it (GPP 6000: 142). This is the point marking the dawn of Ramanuja's *Visishtadvaita*. The teacher Yadava Prakasa is said to have plotted the murder of such an ardent but independent-minded student, but Ramanuja was fortunate to escape the plot and seek guidance from Tirukkachi Nambi in spiritual matters. In this scene Parthasarathy brings the ageing and repentant Yadava to the young and rising pontiff Ramanuja. The philosophical disputes that Ramanuja had as a student over the interpretation of not only the monkey/lotus verse, but also the passage *Satyam Gnanam Anantam Brahma* from *Taittiriya Upanishad* are also alluded to in the soliloquy of Yadava who comes to take refuge in Ramanuja.[2] At this point, for him, the doctrine does not pertain to *what* is Brahman or reality, but who is our stay (*patrukodu*), that is the relative pronoun 'what' shifts to 'who'. We may say this sums up the difference between *Nirgunabrahman* and *Sagunabrahman* (the ultimate reality which is attributeless and that which has form and qualities). The sources point out that Yadava's conversion was the result of his mother's admiration for Ramanuja (GPP 6000: 176–7). Further in this scene we also meet Mudaliyandan, one of Ramanuja's earliest disciples. His original name was Dasarathi and he was Ramanuja's sister's son. He was put in charge of the temple when Ramanuja undertook a tour of India. Carman (1974) points out that although as a sanyasi Ramanuja had renounced family, he had retained some of his relatives in key positions, not only for their spirit of dedication, but also for their utility in the complex affairs of managing a religious organization. In this scene, the older generation of preceptors is represented not only by Tirukkachi Nambi but also Tiruvaranga Perumal Araiyar, the Cantor in Srirangam Temple. The latter comes to Kanchi to call upon Ramanuja to take up Alavandar's seat at the Srirangam mutt. Parthasarathy employs the *deus ex machina* as it is used in the sources when the Cantor asks Lord Varadaraja for a boon which turns out to be Ramanuja himself. In the sources, the voice of the Lord is heard by everyone, and Ramanuja has to leave Kanchi.

---

[2]See ibid.

ACT II

SCENE 1

The scene is located in Srirangam and, by this time, Ramanuja is a middle-aged man, the pontiff of the Sri Vaishnava mutt there, surrounded by senior and junior disciples, followers and mentors. For example, Periya Nambi and Maraner Nambi are disciples of Alavandar while Kuresar, Mudaliyandan, and Kidambi Achan are the chief disciples of Ramanuja among the younger generation.

In Tamil Nadu, the term 'Kovil' in Vaishanava parlance invariably refers to the Sri Ranganatha temple at Srirangam. One of the interesting dimensions of Ramanuja's life is his impressive organizing ability. He was not only a pontiff and an acharya who engaged in metaphysical and religious *vichara* or inquiry, but was also a shrewd and efficient manager of mundane matters relating to the running of a temple with all its orthodoxies and complexities. *Guruparamparai Prabhavam* narrates how he went to Srirangam, entered the temple, took charge, presided over the gathering of temple officials, checked the treasury, verified whether all the services were being performed without compromise, looked into discrepancies and discriminations among the various folds of functionaries, got the ramparts repaired, surpervised the maintenance of gardens, and appointed as supervisor the chieftain Akalanga Nattazhwar. He saw to it that all festivals were conducted in accordance with the regulations laid down (GPP 6000: 184). The Tamil biographer S. Kalyanarama Iyengar (1978: Ch. 17) gives a synopsis of the reforms that Ramanuja executed at Srirangam temple. We find some interesting features in Ramanuja's distribution of work. The administration of the inner shrine had ten divisions (*kothu*) which were entrusted to Brahmins. The outer administration of the rest of the temple too had ten divisions which were managed by Sudras or non-Brahmins. Iyengar lists the officials put in charge (ibid.: 202–3). Some equally interesting social details may be noted in the distribution: various non-Brahmins and subcastes were each assigned a temple task, be it the agrarian Vellala community or the blacksmiths, the carpenters, or the weavers who had to make fresh cloth for cooking, even the dhobis or laundering community (ibid: 205), the rowers (*odakkarargal*) who had to cross over to the other side of river Kaveri during floods to bring provisions for the temple, etc. According to his order, the tenfold Sudra officials, as well as other upper-caste non-Brahmin merchants, in fact every group, had a designated privilege of serving the temple (ibid.: 256). An important record of the various changes and reforms in administering the big temple in Srirangam is a work in Tamil called *Kovil Ozhugu* (The Conduct of the Affairs of the Temple). Although Ramanuja stepped into the shoes of Alavandar, all the traditional sources note how he faced tremendous opposition from the hereditary managers of the temple and how he carefully went about reorganizing the establishment. He was aware of the caste dynamics operating in the Hindu temple system. He tried to remove certain corrupt officials and switch castes in certain positions. Wherever there was resistance, he maintained the status quo. In this difficult job of taking over the temple management and handling intrigues and subversions, he was ably assisted by the most intelligent of his disciples, Kuresa. The chief or high priest of the temple was Thiruvarangathu Amudhanar. It is recorded that the chief priest resisted Ramanuja's reformist moves and even Lord Ranganatha appeared in Ramanuja's dream and asked him not to touch him. Ramanuja almost gave up the idea of dismissing the chief priest, but it was Kuresa who deployed a series of stratagems to bring around the rebellious priest and his followers. All the sources record this embarrassing episode in Ramanuja's career, some in a favourable light, some in a neutral tone. It is said that during the obsequies for his mother, the chief priest invited Kuresa on the eleventh day to be the Brahmin guest. The mother, when she was alive, had become fond of Kuresa reciting the *prabandhams* and *pasurams* and he, thereby, had endeared himself to the lady. Perhaps for this reason the chief priest might have called him to act as the ritual guest to please his mother's spirit. Kuresa used this opportunity to corner the chief priest. When the time came after the feast for the host to ritually ask the guest whether he was satisfied, the guest instead of replying '*truptosmi*' (I am satisfied), as he was supposed to, kept mum. When pressed by the priest to say what would satisfy him, Kuresa asked for the keys of the temple and the chief priest was completely stunned. But he had no option because of the ritual compulsion and he surrendered the keys. Kuresa promptly handed them over to his guru Ramanuja. The sources also narrate how the chief priest abruptly left Srirangam for his village where he completed the remaining rituals. Later, he became one of Ramanuja's disciples and was given the name 'Amudhanar', meaning one who is as sweet as nectar. He composed a panegyric in praise of Ramanuja in Tamil called *Ramanuja Nutrandadi* (anthology of hundred verses on Ramanuja). Analysing this intriguing change of equations, Carman surmises that it would not have been an amicable situation for either party. He makes the incisive comment that 'it is remarkable that ... Ramanuja should have been praised by the man whose authority in the temple he had so seriously diminished' (Carman 1974: 36). He also mentions in a footnote that a different version of the episode was given by the descendants of the chief priest in Srirangam, when an earlier western researcher, Walter G. Neevel Jr., in the company of K.K.A. Venkatachari, went to interview them in 1968. They alleged that Ramanuja had even tried to poison their ancestor (ibid.: 281, fn. 24).

In the play, surprisingly, Parthasarathy simply eulogizes the encounter between Ramanuja and the chief priest. It is made out in the scene as though the chief priest willingly surrendered the keys. However, there is no doubt that Ramanuja was a reformer who wanted to redefine the temple-centred life which was the axle of the wheel of Hindu society. Ramanuja wanted to follow an assimilationist policy by bringing about a friendly interaction between the various castes of society. In this he was convinced that he was continuing the legacy left by Alavandar. This is the true meaning of '*Guruparampara*'. The lofty ideal of placing the Vaishnava mutt beyond caste and gender discrimination is articulated eloquently in this scene by Ramanuja. He declares that the temple festival is a community celebration and that the deity would be taken around in procession in all the streets, not just in the upper-caste quarters.

Another important contribution of the Vaishnava acharyas from Nathamuni onwards was the upholding of the *Nalayira Divya Prabandham* in Tamil to be as sacred as the Vedas, and hence according it the status of scripture. Nathamuni is said to be the one who set these hymns to music. Legend has it that Nathamuni was very much captivated by the snatches of the hymns he heard sung by a group of devotees from the uplands at the temple at Veeranarayanapuram. The Lord Mannanar later commanded him to set them to music. In obedience to this, he set the prabandhas to music with the help of his nephews. Alkondavilli Govindacharya notes that 'Prabandhas being now like the Vedas, associated with the three fold intonation of *Udátta, Anudátta* and *Svarita*, spread, from that time onwards, far and wide in the land' (AKVG 1906 [2004: 5]). They came to be called *devagana* or celestial music. It is well known that the Vedas have a distinct *chanda* or measure and the Tamil hymnal writings have a completely different metre and mode of reciting. The credit for arranging for Tamil hymns to be recited in the Srirangam temple goes to Nathamuni and Tiruvaranga Perumal Araiyar, the latter having specialized in this performance. Carman aptly calls him the Cantor. Ramanuja continued this practice with greater vigour. In fact, after he fled to Karnataka, at a late age in his life, he also introduced the practice of reciting the pasurams of the Azhwars and the prabandhas in Vishnu temples in that region, especially Melukote. The epigraphist B.R. Gopal has provided inscriptional evidence to confirm how, soon after Ramanuja's time, there were donors and donatrixes who created endowments for this purpose. Such donations increased in number in the thirteenth and fourteenth centuries.[3] The term *Ubhaya Vedanta* refers to a scholar who is equally proficient and knowledgeable in Sanskrit and Tamil. Ramanuja himself may be considered one such *Ubhayavedanti*. Culturally speaking, his praise of Tamil also throws light on the tension between the two linguistic groups in South India—the hegemonic Sanskrit tradition and the Dravidian tradition led by Tamil. However, there is no recorded evidence that Ramanuja wrote anything in Tamil, although a number of statements are attributed to him in the oral tradition. Indira Parthasarathy's Ramanuja throws the privilege of reading the scripture open to all.

Ramanuja finds spirituality synonymous with beauty. Hence bhakti is an aesthetic rasa or experience. We recall that Ramanuja was so humble that he was only too eager to learn various types of scriptural and devotional literature from the chief disciples of Alavandar. In fulfilment of Alavandar's wish, he was to learn from five teachers—*panchacharya padasrita* (Kalyanarama Iyengar 1978: 108). We have already noted his efforts to learn from Tirukkachi

---

[3]See The Point of View of the Epigrapher in 'Hagiography Revisited'.

Nambi and Periya Nambi. Now he is directed to go to Thirukottiyur, which is a temple town lying between Sivaganga and Tirupathur, on the banks of river Manimutharu. A well-read scholar of the Vedas, the Upanishads and the *Gita*, named Thirukottiyur Nambi, was residing in this town. In Sanskrit his name is Ghoshti Purna, which means a leader around whom a spiritually inclined group has gathered (ibid.: 97).

SCENE 2

Scene 2 dramatizes an episode that is a favourite with every biographer and hagiographer of Ramanuja, namely his defying the great Vedic scholar Ghoshti Purna. Tradition says that Ramanuja went eighteen times all the way from Srirangam to Tirukottiyur travelling about 130 miles, begging Ghoshti Purna to teach him the secret doctrines of Vaishnava texts, particularly the *Ashtakshari* (the eight-syllabled mantra *Om Namo Narayanaya*) and the *Dvaya mantra* (*Sriman Narayana—Charanau Saranam Prabadhye Srimathe Narayanaya Namaha*) uttering which a true Vaishnava can attain heavenly abode. Some of the biographers describe Ramanuja as an exemplary and obedient student. He strictly followed the restrictions and discipline pertaining to food, speech, and other aspects that Ghoshti Purna mercilessly imposed on him to try his mettle and test the keenness of his aspiration. The Tamil biographer Kalyanarama Iyengar describes the event and the mental make-up of Ghoshti Purna with a touch of irony. Perhaps Ghoshti Purna was somewhat hard-hearted. Maybe it justified because one cannot simply give away a precious treasure. How was it possible to give it all away without a price? The tests to which Ramanuja was subjected have been wittily compared by the biographer to a modern-day examination to secure a professional position, not to speak of recommendation from higher ups (Kalyanarama Iyengar 1978: 112)!

As a young seeker Ramanuja's dialogue with the learned Ghoshti Purna is interesting. He professes his ambition to write a commentary on the *Vyasasutras* as desired by the late lamented Alavandar. Ghoshti Purna is perhaps sceptical. But Ramanuja persists in his plea on the grounds that he should acquire the qualifications and credentials necessary for a mutt's head. This is what in Sri Vaishnava scriptural tradition is called *Adhikaratvam*, that is the eligibility to do or learn something. S. Kalyanarama Iyengar expands the cryptic explanation in *Guruparamparai Prabhavam* of the significance of the utterances of Ghoshti Purna during the eighteen times Ramanuja sought him. i) An aspirant (*mumukshu*) should annul attachment to worldly pursuits; ii) with the rise of goodness, the ego and a sense of ownership will vanish; iii) unless and until the ego and sense of ownership get dissolved, attention to the body will not vanish; iv) unless and until attachment to the body perishes, self-knowledge will not arise; v) unless and until knowledge of the self is born, disdain or hatred of worldly prosperity (*upekshai*) will not cease; vi) unless and until the cessation of worldly attachment happens; devotion to God will not be born; vii) unless and until devotion to God arises, the taste for worldly enjoyment will not be extinguished; viii) unless and until the taste for worldly enjoyment ceases, one's sense of dependence on God (*paratantriyam*) will not be born; ix) unless and until one understands one's dependence on God, attachment to material possessions and worldly passions and hatred will not die; x) unless and until one becomes free from likes and dislikes, one will not attain the state of a Sri Vaishnava (that is one who will not brook another man's misery); xi) unless and until one attains the state of a Sri Vaishnava, one will not get acceptance among and accessibility to the fold of good (*satwic*) people; xii) unless and until one gets admission into the fold of satwic people, acceptance from devotees of the Lord (*bhāgavata parigraham*) will not be possible; xiii) unless and until one gets acceptance from the fold of devotees, one cannot hope for close proximity to the Lord (*bhagavata parigraham*); xiv) unless and until one attains proximity to the Lord, one will not turn Godward in one's pursuits (*ananya prayojanam*); xv) unless and until one turns Godward, one will not understand one's worthiness to be dependent on God alone; xvi) unless and until one understands one's dependence on God alone, one will not understand that there is no other refuge for one (*ananyarha seshabhutan*); xvii) unless and until one understands that there is no refuge but God (*ananyasaranagatan*), one will not become eligible for initiation (*adhikari purushan*); xviii) the inner import of the Ashtakhari mantra will be realized only by an eligible person.

Ghoshti Purna directs Ramanuja to come by himself the eighteenth time. But Ramanuja chooses to go with Kuresa and Mudaliyandan. When Ghoshti Purna reprimands him for violating his injunction, Ramanuja gives the famous reply: Kuresa is his pennant (*pavitram*) and Mudaliyandan his staff (*dandam*). These are the two insignia of a Vaishnavite *sanyasi* or renunciate. According to the sources, the encounter with Ghoshti Purna also brought immortal fame to Ramanuja because when he was initiated into the sacred mantras which guaranteed salvation, the young and noble Ramanuja thought of sharing this supreme knowledge with as many people as possible. Prompted by this urge, he is said to have climbed up to the second balcony of the inner tower of the local temple of Lord Saumyanarayana, called the people to gather around, and initiated them into the secret mantra. This particular act of the warm-hearted Ramanuja has so inspired generations of biographers and hogiographers that they have made it the very centre of Ramanuja's entire life and career. It has been held that Ramanuja was the only acharya of the ancient Hindu tradition to have invited the whole of humanity to share in the privilege of salvation through uttering the sacred mantras. His action is constantly cited as exemplifying his egalitarianism, humanism, and compassion for others. Hence, in some of the accounts, he is said to have climbed up the outer tower of the temple and called out to all. Carman thinks that the incident of Ramanuja going up the staircase and hailing the others must surely have happened and even the spirit of exaggeration and the accretions to the event can be understood in the light of the eagerness to project him as a great modern teacher. S. Kalyanarama Iyengar gives a detailed picture of the structure of this particular temple after sketching its local lore. The central portion over the sanctum has a tower called *Ashtanga Vimanam* (eight-faceted). The uppermost level is called 'heaven' where the Lord is in standing position. In the southern stretch of the same level we have an image of Ramanuja holding his hand in the posture of initiating someone. At the middle level, the Lord is in a sitting posture. At the first or lowest level, the Lord is in a recumbent posture. Devotees are allowed to climb all the three tiers. Parthasarathy also makes Ramanuja in this scene a modern-day Ambedkar-like leader who has a social goal to achieve, namely dissolving caste distinctions and opening up scriptural learning to all. In this scene, Ramanuja explains the secret of Ashtakshari and declares his socio-spiritual motive. Carman, however, wonders about the social composition of the congregation which heard

Ramanuja's explanation of the *mantra*, Om Namo Narayanaya. At that point of time, temples were not open to the lower castes of Hindu society. Perhaps his listeners would mostly have been Brahmins and other upper caste Hindus (Carman 1974: 40). Even so, it does not take away from the greatness of Ramanuja's thinking. Even his preceptor Ghoshti Purna recognized the large-heartedness of the young Ramanuja.[4]

SCENE 3

This scene depicts the hostility of the orthodox devotees and priests of the Srirangam temple towards Ramanuja. Parthasarathy combines different episodes from the sources and constructs a very effective scene of confrontation between the progressive school of Vaishnavism represented by Ramanuja, his mentor Periya Nambi and his daring daughter Attuzhi on the one hand, and on the other, the diehard orthodoxy of those days represented by characters who are not given any names but simply called Brahmins 1, 2, 3, and 4. Parthasarathy is highly skilled in dramatizing the power motivation in human beings and its subtle as well as crude manifestations in specific social milieus. There are several aspects of intercaste and intra-caste encounter which the scene brilliantly captures. As for the Brahmins, there is, among those from the southern districts, a suspicion of Ramanuja who hails from a northern district of the Tamil country. There is also contempt for his idea of Vaishnavism because he sought instruction from a non-Brahmin teacher. Exploiting the legend that the illustrious Brahmin Acharya Alavandar took an outcaste Maraner Nambi as his disciple, the playwright forges an eloquent scene involving Periya Nambi, Maraner Nambi, Ramanuja, and the Brahmins. In the source narrative, Maraner Nambi was stricken with an incurable disease and was nursed by Periya Nambi. This is briefly mimed in the scene. However, in the source when Maraner Nambi died Periya Nambi decided to accord him the funeral rites which are normally performed for only a dead Brahmin. There is a profoundly interesting exchange between Ramanuja and Periya Nambi in the source at this point. Ramanuja is startled by the radicalism of Maha

---

[4]See The Life of Ramanuja in History and Legend in 'Hagiography Revisited'.

Purna's thinking and action. He fears that such a subversive move might destroy the very fabric of Hindu society. He tells his teacher that while he was doing everything to keep the fence intact, Maha Purna was doing away with it. To this Maha Purna gives an eloquent reply.[5] In a virtual peroration, he recalls all the great sages, seers, kings and ministers in Indian tradition who had not been Brahmins, for example Veda Vyasa, the sage and Vidura the wise minister of the Kurus in the Mahabharata. But in the play all the enlightened ideas and utterances of Maha Purna are virtually transferred to Ramanuja. Ramanuja supports Maha Purna's efforts to protect Maraner Nambi from the wrath of the Brahmins and even challenges them. Thus the play reverses the roles of Ramanuja and Maha Purna as we find them in the hagiographies.[6] In this scene Maraner Nambi is alive and Ramanuja proclaims the universality of his Vaishnava dharma. If the sources view Ramanuja as one who does not engage in violent subversion but aims at persuading people to think with sweetness and enlightenment, Parthasarathy gives a subversive and iconoclastic edge to everything that Ramanuja says and does.

Another deliberate departure that the play makes is in the prominence given to Maha Purna's daughter Attuzhay. In the source she is a timid, weak girl who could not face her mother-in-law's taunts. Ramanuja had to send his nephew and prime disciple Dasarathi as a domestic help (*seedhana vellatti*) to help her.

In this dramatic version, there is a fresh textual moment created by Parthasarathy when, as a young woman, Attuzhay dares to confront the orthodox Brahmins and even halt the procession of the deity. Parthasarathy is at his theatrical best in such scenes which dismantle received social structures. Not only are the orthodox Brahmins and their ugly intrigues exposed by the young woman, but they are also driven into a corner when she appeals directly to Lord Ranganatha Himself to expose the villainy of his so-called pious priests. Using the time-tested theatrical technique of the *deus ex machina* the playwright makes the Lord Himself indict the wicked Brahmins. However, Parthasarathy follows the sources closely in the

---

[5] See The Place of Ramanuja in Indian Thought and Cultural History and also A Critique of the Play *Ramanujar* in 'Hagiography Revisited'.

[6] See 'Life of Ramanuja in History and Legend in 'Hagiography Revisited'.

employment of this device because in the sources the Lord always speaks through the priest. The term used for this mode is *Archaka Mukena*, meaning, as Carman points out, 'through the priest'. Parthasarathy's purpose here is very different. The ordinary folk who come to the defence of the beleaguered Attuzhai are regarded by her as the voice of the Lord. In fact, the priests here engage in double dealing by pretending to praise and support her; when the Brahmins are outraged, the priests reveal a stratagem to do away with Ramanuja, who is the source of all the trouble. The scene recalls the brilliant dramatic power which is all pervasive in another of Parthasarathy's plays, *Nandan Kathai*. The use of stichomythic dialogue, is characteristic of the playwright. It serves to highlight the conspiracy that is brewing to eliminate Ramanuja. The motive of the Brahmins ironically is to sustain *Manusmriti*, which has canonized *Varnasrama dharma*, that is the perpetuation of caste hierarchy.

Tiruppaanazhwar (eighth century AD) was found as a child in a paddy field by a man belonging to the untouchable community (Panan) and brought up by him. He grew up as a devotee of the Lord of Srirangam but, since he could not enter the precincts of the temple or even the temple town, he used to stand on the southern bank of the river Kaveri and sing hymns in praise of Lord Ranga. One day, rapt in the ecstasy of devotional fervour, he did not notice or hear Lokasaranga, a Brahmin priest, carrying water from the river for Lord Ranganatha and shouting to the untouchable Pana to move away. The Brahmin priest threw a stone at Pana which hit the latter on the forehead and caused bleeding. Pana meekly moved away but when Lokasaranga went into the shrine, he found Lord Ranganatha's forehead bleeding. The Lord then appeared in Lokasaranga's dream that night and bade him carry Pana on his shoulders and bring him to the inner shrine of the temple. Lokasaranga carried out the Lord's command, in spite of Pana's remonstrances. According to legend, Pana, his ardent desire to see the Lord's beatific form now fulfilled, merged into the Lord forever. He was canonized as Tiruppaanazhwar. The ten pasurams that he sang in praise of Lord Ranganatha, which were included in the *Nalayira Divya Prabandham*, are known as *Amalanadipiran*.

SCENE 4

This scene virtually repeats the source narratives in their details. However, it underscores Ramanuja's openness of mind with regard to people, their caste, their complexion, their social position. It also brings in the temple intrigues to poison Ramanuja who goes on his customary rounds, begging for food as a sanyasi. On the one hand, there is the purity of soul that Urangavilli possesses and on the other there are the sinister machinations of the temple power group. Further, Urangavilli's total devotion and the even greater devotion of his wife Ponnachi are in sharp contrast to the unenlightened behaviour of Ramanuja's own Brahmin disciples. Three-fourths of the scene, which very close to the sources, serves to reiterate Indira Parthasarathy's objective in the play, namely to highlight Ramanuja's reformist zeal to transcend caste barriers. According to caste regulations, a Brahmin acharya can lean on anybody before a bath, but after bathing, only on a Brahmin. Ramanuja deliberately reverses this dictum and leans on the 'purest' of his Brahmin disciples Kuresa (in the sources, on Mudaliyandan, GPP 6000: 236) before his bath in the river Kaveri, but on the non-Brahmin Urangavilli, after the bath. This puzzles his disciples no end. Ramanuja's reply in the original narratives underscores the need to avoid pride on account of one's high caste (GPP 6000: 236). One of the aspects we notice about Ramanuja's spiritual academy is that he does not forbid any of his disciples from asking unsettling questions; because he is open as a guru, he feels no embarrassment. His disciples are invited to challenge even their own master. Indira Parthasarathy has created a hilarious farce out of this episode, but it is also thought-provoking. Ramanuja declares once again his conception of a Vaishnava society which does not distinguish between a Brahmin and a warrior (*Marava*) which Urgangavilli is.

SCENE 5

It has been mentioned in all the accounts that Ramanuja gave a prominent place to women in his mutt. We have already seen the leading role that Attuzhay plays in containing the power of the conspiring Brahmins of the temple. Again Ponnachi in the last scene showed how a woman can be spiritually pure and capable of complete surrender.

In this scene, we have one more woman—Paruthikkollai near Tirupati who shows extraordinary understanding of Ramanuja's ideals. Indira Parthasarathy uses the scene to underscore the point that one need not be a Brahmin nor be 'chaste' in a conventional sense to be a Vaishnavite. Ramanuja has no sense of false propriety either. Even the lascivious merchant who tries to blackmail Paruthikkollai is reformed by her inner sense of chastity and her dedication to higher truths. Ramanuja at the end of the scene praises him for his fairness and decency which has prompted him to act according to his dharma as a Vaisya (belonging to the merchant class) whereas Ramanuja's own disciples have no such credentials. Mere caste superiority in social organization cannot be used to claim superiority for the upper castes. This is certainly crucial to Ramanuja's reinterpretation of Varnasrama dharma.

SCENE 6

Scene 6 is again important from the point of view of Ramanuja's recognition of gender equality. Here we have Andal Amma, wife of Kuresa, who is as well read and of as high intellectual calibre as her husband. That is the reason why she is sitting with him in compliance with Ramanuja's instruction when the acharya is dictating his magnum opus *Sri Bhashyam* on Vyasa's *Brahmasutra*. In fact, Indira Parthasarathy makes a departure here from the sources. In the sources Andal Amma is merely present during this dictatation. But in the play and in this scene, she is actively involved in the philosophical discussion regarding the nature of consciousness. In fact, none of the so-called disciples of Ramanuja is given such recognition by the guru.

The scene is also important from the point of view of the philosophical basis of Ramanuja's school of Vaishnavism. The reigning Indian metaphysical thought in those times was *Advaita* which had found its redoubtable proponent and commentator in Adi Sankara, a few centuries before Ramanuja. Advaita is described as 'monism' because the term 'a-dvaita' means non-duality. The kernel question in Hindu metaphysics is, is there any reality inhering in the universe? Advaita holds that the world is 'maya' (illusion) and self or consciousness alone is real: '*brahma satyam jagan mitya*'. Further, it rejects the notion that God or Brahman has any attributes, that is *gunas*. Ramanuja, while dictating his *bhashya* or exegesis, comes to this crux. He, for some reason, continues in the vein of Advaita and asks Kuresa to write that the soul is marked by self-consciousness. At this point Kuresa, in conformity with their agreement, stops writing because he disagrees with Ramanuja's explanation that the self or consciousness is sufficient unto itself. Earlier Ramanuja had dictated views apparently countering the Advaitic position, arguing that there is a meaningful relationship between *Isvara* or the Lord and the created universe. For the self or the soul, the Lord is the frontier land of all meanings and purposes. Having said that, when he goes on to designate the self as oriented towards itself, he seems to be shaking the very base of his school of thought which he has inherited from Nathamuni through Alavandar by taking instruction from the five chief disciples of the latter. It is intriguing at this point that Ramanuja should state that the body is merely an inert object and it is only through *gnana* or consciousness that we develop a sense of attributes. Kuresa legitimately refuses to proceed as an amanuensis because this view of the relationship between *chit* and *achit* (consciousness and matter) vis-à-vis Isvara (the Lord) militates against the Vaishnava understanding of the nature of *Brahman* and the self. Carman, looking at this apparent lapse on the part of Ramanuja as a thinker of the *Visishtadvaita* school, surmises that Ramanuja's turning towards the concept of the Lord with attributes of perfection (*Sagunabrahman*) as opposed to the Advaitic concept of attributeless Brahman (*Nirguna Brahman*) must have happened gradually and not at a moment of sudden revelation or conversion (Carman 1974: 97). Ramanuja was himself born in the Somayaji Vadama Brahmin community and even his initial training was under the great teacher of Advaita, Yadava Prakasa. It is likely that Ramanuja was automatically explaining the Brahman/ the self as contentless consciousness. It is only logical that Kuresa should register his protest at the conception of the human soul as self-existing, because such an idea is anathema to a Vaishnava. If granted, it will negate the value of surrender to the Divine which has been conceptualized at various levels as *prapatti*, *saranagati*, and in general called *bhakti*. Ramanuja comes to realize the grave error that he has committed and steers himself back onto the right path of interpretation. This is interestingly dramatized in this scene, with Ramanuja asking Andal Amma to indicate where he went wrong. It shows his respect for her intellectual acumen and power of discrimination. In his characteristic intertextual style, Indira Parthasarathy makes Andal Amma quote, by way of answer, the verse which is part of a similar colloquy between Madhurakavi Azhwar and Nammazhwar about Brahman (reality). This verse, which is in the form of a riddle, makes Ramanuja realize where he has gone wrong. It is this humility, which has been remarked on by all biographers, that makes Ramanuja seek forgiveness of Kuresa. Ramanuja continues the commentary consulting Andal Amma in between. In the source, it is mentioned that when Kuresa did not budge, Ramanuja kicked him (GPP 6000: 223). Indira Parthasarathy omits this very human detail because it may be embarrassing, given the status of Ramanuja as an acharya.

Carman rightly observes that Kuresa was not only Ramanuja's disciple but a collaborator in most of the critical commentarial writings and the other projects that Ramanuja undertook. It has also been pointed out that Ramanuja completed the *Sri Bhashyam* after he returned from his exile in the Karnataka region for more than a decade. Kuresa himself had left Srirangam (obviously ostracized by the orothdox Brahmin community) to live in Tirumalirunjolai near Madurai and returned to Srirangam only after Ramanuja himself came back. The *Sri Bhashyam* must have been resumed and completed by Ramanuja during the last few years of his life with the help of Kuresa, who had been blinded earlier.

ACT III

SCENE 1

This scene is testimony to Indira Pathasarathy's brilliant dramatic powers. As a playwright and theatre artist, his forte is pungent satire and cryptic stichomythic dialogue, invariably employed in situations of intrigue and cunning. In *Nandan Kathai*, there are any number of such instances where Parthasarathy exposes the lust for power in human nature which conceals itself under the garb of religious piety and orthodoxy. He depicts in this scene how disgruntled Vaishnava Brahmins, Saivite Brahmins, and non-Brahmins collude with each other to devise a stratagem to get Ramanuja deported. This is very much reminiscent of the conspiracy hatched by the upper caste Hindus in *Nandan Kathai* to eliminate the rising and devout pariah Nandan. In this play on Ramanuja, Indira Parthasarathy structures the dialogue in such a manner that all those who are opposed to the progressive measures of Ramanuja in throwing open the temple to the fifth and untouchable caste, betray themselves by their own utterances. They mock at his high moral and spiritual ground and his respect for the lower castes. Although in the medieval Tamil country, there was bitter intra-religious animosity between the Vaishnavites and Saivites, what puts them on the same axis here is the fear of the rising prestige of Ramanuja. The Vaishnavites are those whose interests have in some way been injured by Ramanuja's temple reforms. They are willing to join hands with their arch-enemies the Saivites, in inciting the Chola king against Ramanuja. One should say that here Indira Parthasarathy has created a brilliant 'writerly' text out of the sources.

SCENE 2

This short scene develops the conspiracy of the previous scene by bringing the subject of the danger of allowing Ramanuja's stature to grow, right into the king's court. Ramanuja and his mutt are betrayed by none other than Kuresa's disciple Naluran. The king is instigated by the disgruntled Brahmins through Naluran, but the persecution of Ramanuja by a Chola king is still an undecided matter and has provoked a lot of historical debate as recently as 2002. The biographies and Vaishnavite sectarian accounts mention the Chola king, but nowhere is it clear who that king.[7]

But Parthasarathy is not willing to give credence to rabid sectarian theories. In his view, the king was neutral, perhaps more balanced than the warring groups. However, being in power, no monarch could ignore religious forces as is borne out even today by contemporary politics. The king orders Ramanuja to be brought to the court. Note that it is not the king who orders the arrest of Ramanuja but only Naluran who has a personal grouse against

---

[7] See History and Hagiographer in 'Hagiography Revisited'.

Ramanuja's moves to reform temple administration. Indira Parthasarathy thus brings out the political dimensions of religion in this scene as well as the next. Religion, power, and politics have been located in the same grid, in earlier epochs too as in our times. Indira Parthasarathy wants to demystify the hagiographic image of religion which tends to dissemble the political.

SCENE 3

There is an atmosphere of menace with the soldiers breaking into the precincts of Ramanuja's mutt in Srirangam. However, as the sources have recorded, Kuresa intervenes with great alacrity and impersonates Ramanuja, wearing the latter's saffron robes. It is touching that the aged Maha Purna also insists on accompanying him, sending a message to Ramanuja to flee from the Tamil country. There is no abstract projection of evil. On the other hand, Indira Parthasarathy makes a nuanced presentation. For example, the soldiers are reluctant to apprehend a sanyasi and are critical of Naluran. Ramanuja is presented in a very human light when confronted by this unexpected turn of events. He is, indeed, upset by Kuresa's move. But Andal Amma reminds Ramanuja that he is not an individual but an institution and has a responsibility to society. Indira Parthasarathy thus makes Andal Amma a strong woman in the face of danger to her own husband in this politically unsettling situation. Ramanuja leaves the mutt in the hands of Andal Amma, a move which is not found recorded in the sources. As in the case of Attuzhay, Indira Parthasarathy gives a more enabling role to another woman, Andal Amma. Ramanuja reluctantly decides to run north-west, to the Nilgiri mountains. However, we notice that he has already had profound impact on people living in regions away from Srirangam so that there is sure to be help and refuge. There is a reference to one Nallan Chakravarty who became a devotee of Ramanuja. Unlike orthodox Brahmins, he had followed the noble precepts of Ramanuja, and treated tribals and non-Brahmins in his region with respect and kindness. He had, like Maha Purna, performed obsequies meant for a Brahmin for a fifth caste non-Brahmin. He was excommunicated by the townfolk, but the Lord Himself praised him declaring, 'In the eyes of the world you are a bad man; but to me you are a good man'

(AKVG 1906[2004]: 152). Indira Parthasarathy follows the source in this because it serves his purpose of highlighting the values of the new Vaishnavism which is emerging, effacing the stigma of caste from Hinduism.

SCENE 4

This court scene does not seem to have any recorded historical source, although all the hagiographic narratives make a dramatic situation out of the Chola persecution of Kuresa and Maha Purna. The important departure by Indira Parthasarathy from all such sources is that he does not present the king as a wicked, rabid, religious fundamentalist. In Indira Parthasarathy's view, the king is neutral like Pontius Pilate who was compelled by the Jews to persecute Jesus Christ. Naluran is the Judas who betrays Ramanuja. The playwright tries to suggest that no king can afford to antagonize the powerful religious groups in his country. When the king comes to know that Ramanuja has fled the country, he is not inclined to pursue him. But Naluran compels him to take action against Kuresa who has impersonated Ramanuja. The scene certainly belongs to Kuresa who outwits Naluran by a quibble which suggests that a measure called *dronam* is bigger than another measure *sivam*: '*Sivatparadaram nasti? dronamasti tatparam*' (GPP 6000: 256). The Bengali biographer Swami Ramakrishnananda explains that as units of measure dronam is 32 seers while sivam is one half of that weight (1899 [1959: 209]). He offers a fine interpretation saying that Kuresa ridiculed the pundits' attempt to set limits to God who is limitless, immeasurable. In the hagiographical narratives, the king gets angry with the quick wit of Kuresa and orders him to be blinded. But in the play the king is reluctant to act. In one version, Kuresa and Maha Purna are blinded by the soldiers. But in most versions, they blind themselves which they deem an honourable act. Maha Purna dies after walking some distance, near Pasupati Kolil (AKVG 1906[2004: 173]). Kuresa proceeds to Srirangam. Ramanuja makes a distinction between a man who has the Vaishnava spirit and a man who is merely born in a Vaishnava family. It is crucial to know that birth is not the sole criterion of superiority.

Kuresa has attained glory in the history of Sri Vaishnava religion as one who gave his '*darsana*' (sight) for the sake of '*darsana*' (vision/

faith). The *Guruparamparai Prabhavam* narrates how he scraped out his eyes using his 'blessed nails', feeling happy that 'I am fortunate to give up my sight for the faith which is verily vision' (GPP 6000: 256). The epigrammatic brevity of the Tamil utterance and the profound play on the word 'darsana' by repetition cannot, however, be captured in English.

SCENE 5

It is Ramanuja's experience of exile and the necessity to seek assistance from people living away from towns and established societies that causes his consciousness to expand. His exile is a blessing in disguise. Among the acharyas of mainstream Hinduism, it was Ramanuja who took cognizance of the social space within which people have to operate. He has already shown a natural readiness to be open-minded and has been capable of recognizing innate spirituality, as in the case of the couple Urangavilli and Ponnachi. In this scene, he comes across hunters when he flees into the forest. The Indian social organization had kept tribals and forest dwellers outside its pale. However, there was interaction between the various groups depending upon the circumstances. In this scene, we have a reference to one Nallan Chakravarty who was a devotee of Ramanuja and who took kindly to the hunters and initiated them into Vaishnavism. Although there is no specific historical record for it, the Vaishnava hagiographic literature describes such legends. Vaishnavism today is widespread even among tribals, besides upper and lower caste Hindus. In the play, Ramanuja actually embraces one of the hunters notwithstanding the fact that physical touching of a lower caste Hindu was considered polluting. In the sources, hunters bring fruit and honey to Ramanuja, but no cooked food, as noted earlier.

Historically speaking, Ramanuja's moving towards Tondanur in the Karnataka region is socially and religiously significant. B.R. Gopal, the editor of *Epigraphia Carnatica* Vol.VI, has endeavoured to provide epigraphical confirmation of Ramanuja's sojourn in Karnataka and his effort to spread the Sri Vaishnava faith in the Mysore region. In his later book, *Sri Ramanuja in Karnataka* (1983), Gopal points out that Tondanur, also called Tonnur, has a Narasimha temple which is an old one and Ramanuja must have stayed there. It was a capital or capital outpost of the Hoysalas. Looking at the etymology of the word 'Tondanur' Gopal notes that it is a Dravidian, specifically Tamil, word, deriving from the root *tondu* which means service to the Lord by a devotee who is a *dasan*, that is slave. Its original name was Yadavapura, capital of Vishnuvardhana in 1129. The name Tondanur appears in the records of the twelfth century and more in those of the thirteenth century. Yadavapura became Tondanur when Ramanuja settled down there with devotees and servants (Gopal 1983: 14). This fact offers indirect evidence of Ramanuja's stay in Tondanur. It must have been so named owing to his influence. The sources say that there was one Tondanur Nambi who was a devotee of Ramanuja though he had not met him earlier. The hunters guide Ramanuja to him. All the legends and an exhaustive modern biography in English like Alkondavilli Govindacharya's *Sri Ramanujacharya* narrate Ramanuja's encounter with the king of the region almost in a uniform way, that is the king Bittaladevan was a Jain and Ramanuja converted him to Vaishnavism and gave him the name Vishnuvardhana. But B.R. Gopal (1983: 15) categorically affirms that 'there is nothing to show, barring traditional, legendary accounts, that Vishnuvardhana was a Jaina by faith'. He cites K.T. Ramaswamy in *The Hoysala Dynasty*, who says that 'the support and sympathy of Vishnuvardhana to the cause of Sri Vaishnavism was interpreted this way. It might be that this might have given rise to a floating tradition about his conversion' (quoted in ibid.: 14). Various epigraphic and historical details show that he was already called Vishnuvardhana, followed a liberal policy in religious matters, and that Bittaladevan is a Kannada derivation of the Sanskrit 'Vishnu' (ibid.: 15). Alkondavilli Govindacharya surprisingly says that Tondanur was inhabited by Buddhists, but B.R. Gopal points out that Ramanuja first came to the villages of Mirle and Saligram which had a strong Jain population. We can note that Sravanabelagola, which is a historic Jain site, is a little above these villages in Hasan district. The local population at Mirle and Saligram must have resisted Ramanuja's entry and expressed displeasure at the new faith. But the sources as well as the play note that the chief motive of Ramanuja was not to convert anybody, he was pressurized by some of the devotees to go to Melukote to meet the king and seek his patronage. Parthasarathy follows the legends about Ramanuja exorcizing the spirit that possessed the king's daughter, which was one of the reasons cited for the king's turning a devotee of Ramanuja and his conversion to Sri Vaishnava faith.

SCENE 6

Although the exorcism of the king's daughter was the ostensible motive for Ramanuja to visit the palace according to legend, B.R. Gopal offers a more rational explanation. He points out that there was undoubtedly tension between the Jains and the newly arrived Sri Vaishnavas in the Hoysala region, but Ramanuja must have found a congenial atmosphere in Karnataka as far as the political situation was concerned and the king too was very much taken by the genial personality of the acharya. This must be the reason why Ramanuja moved into the Tondanur–Melukote area. In this scene, however, the playwright foregrounds once again the leitmotif that religion controls power and that no king can afford to antagonize the majority religious community, here the Jains.

Alkondavilli Govindacharya has an interesting observation about the king Bittaladevan having one finger short. The cutting of his finger was apparently a symbolic acceptance of his subservience to the Muslims who are referred to as *Turushka*, *Emmaduraya*, and so on, in the source narratives. The Jains treat physical deficiency as inauspicious and hence when the king wants to host a banquet in honour of Ramanuja, they refuse to accept his invitation. His maimed hand connotes his maimed authority. In fact 'Bittaladevan' means 'fingerless Lord'! (AKVG 1906 [2004: 154]) In the last part of the scene we note that Ramanuja is indeed progressive, for he does not think that it is human and proper to lock up a young girl in a room just because she has mental problems.

SCENE 7

The exorcizing proper takes place in this scene. However, far from using traditional methods of uttering some esoteric mantra or verse and waving a bunch of neem leaves, or throwing sacred ash over the possessed person, Ramanuja speaks to her in a kind and sweet manner and evokes in her a sense of beauty by talking about various flowers in the garden and, above all, he uses music therapy, so to say, by singing a Tamil hymn from Periyazhwar. The girl is gradually calmed and feels relieved of her stress. Ramanuja humbly attributes the restoration of her mental poise to the efficacy of the Ashtakshari mantra, 'Om

Namo Narayanaya'. The second part of the scene dramatizes the political stress under which the king struggles. The Jain guru engages Ramanuja in a religious debate. While he argues for an idea of God as a subtle force, Ramanuja advances the principle of avatarhood or incarnation. The acharya also highlights the *sowlabhya* or accessibility of Lord Narayana as supreme God. He declares that he employed no black magic to deliver the girl of her condition but only surrendered all responsibility to the Lord. The scene ends on a politico-religious note when the Jain guru excommunicates the king from his religion. The king therefore turns to Ramanuja and declares that he is embracing Vaishnavism voluntarily. Govindacharya narrates the conquest of the Jains, how the Jains rose in revolt against Ramanuja, and how 12,000 of them marched in a body towards the Lord Narasimha temple where the acharya had taken refuge and demanded that he argue with them on matters of religion and philosophy before he interfered with their king. 'Ramanuja, seeing this tremendous onslaught of an infuriated crowd, thought to himself thus: "In order to escape from lightning, I have courted thunder; fearing the scorpion, I have fallen a victim to the fangs of a cobra; breaking away from the fetters, I have thrust myself into stocks" (AKVG 1906 [2004: 155]). This is, in fact, a direct rendering in English of the account in *Guruparamparai Prabhavam* (6000: 248): '*Panneerayiram kshabanar eka kalathil vandhu tharkika thodanga udaiyavarum minnalakku anjubavargal idiyin kayil agapattar polavum, thelukku anji pambin vayil agapattar polavumachuthe*'. The epigraphical account of this episode, cited by B.R. Gopal, is found in the Tonnur Yoganarasimha temple where, in a room to the right of the entrance, there is an image of Ramanuja seated on a serpent, probably installed during a later period, commemorating the defeat in the traditional account by the acharya of the Jain scholars in philosophical disputations (Gopal 1983: 19). However, we note two points: i) The sources say that Ramanuja converted the Hoysala king; ii) The epigraphist B.R. Gopal proves that the king was already called by the name Vishnuvardhana and Vishnu worship was quite common in Karnataka. Hence Ramanuja was received with great fervour. But the special contribution of Ramanuja was to give a new boost to the concept of Vishnu as viewed by the Visishtadavaita school and also establish certain special modes of worship in the temples of Karnataka after the manner followed in the Tamil country. This included certain rituals of worship and services codified by the acharya through his *Nemmappadi* (ibid.: 16).[8]

SCENE 8

According to epigraphic sources, Ramanuja is believed to have moved from Tondanur to Melukote after staying at Tondanur for about six years till 1144–5. Tradition has it that he constructed the Tirunarayana temple at Melukote by clearing the woods with the help of the *Panchamas* and transformed the place into a Sri Vaishnava centre of worship. Melukote, which was on a hilltop, must have had an old temple and Ramanuja must have had some renovation done with the help of King Vishnuvardhana. The present Melukote temple must have been built over the years from the Hoysala period to the eighteenth and nineteenth centuries under the Wodeyars of Mysore kingdom (Gopal 1983: 24–5). The *garbhagruha* and *antarala* must have been the original parts and the style is early Hoysala with more Dravidian features. In this scene, Parthasarathy dramatically presents Ramanuja's search for the old temple. All the sources narrate how the Lord appeared in his dream and directed him to find the temple. B.R. Gopal is of the opinion that these writings are a mixture of fact and fiction. Parthasarathy is interested in showing how Ramanuja won over the fifth caste of Hindu society whose members enthusiastically came forward to clear the forests known as the forests of Yadugiri. Legends are cited to show that in the Hindu epics this place was variously known as Narayanadri in *Krithayuga*, as Vedagiri in *Tretayuga*, as Yadavagiri in *Dwaparayuga*, and as Yatisaila in *Kaliyuga* because Ramanuja was a Yathiraja (king among ascetics) who restored its glory (AKVG 1906 [2004: 161]). When the Panchamas discover some ornaments and eventually the idol, Ramanuja rechristens them the 'Tirukkulattar', that is the clan of Sri or Lakshmi. B.R. Gopal does not find any historical records for this event. But S. Kalyanarama Iyengar cites the historical record of the *Mysore Gazetteer* (1978: 325). Legend has it that outcastes had for centuries enjoyed certain privileges in these temples in Karnataka. Govindacharya cites certain other sources to attest Ramanuja's historic recognition of the untouchables

---

[8]See The Point of view of the Epigrapher in 'Hagiography Revisited'.

(AKVG 1906 [2004: 165]). It is even pointed out that Mahatma Gandhi was inspired by Ramanuja's egalitarianism when he named the pariahs 'Harijans', children of Hari or Vishnu.

SCENE 9

The traditional sources narrate that Ramanuja went all the way to to Delhi the sultan's court to request him to hand over the idol of Sampat Kumara which was kept and adored as a plaything by the sultan's daughter. Ramanuja retrieved this idol which was believed to be the festival deity in the older temple at Melukote and which was among the many objects taken away by the sacking sultan's army. In this scene, Ramanuja meets the sultan (who is merely called 'Turkish king'), and persuades him with even tenor and spiritual simplicity, to allow him access to the inner quarters of the princess, where normally no man is allowed, least of all a Hindu *sadhu* regarded as a *kafir*. Legend has that when he called out to Sampat Kumara, the deity jumped down and came and sat on his lap (GPP 6000: 253). Hence he was named 'Chellapillai', meaning 'darling', variously spelt as Chelvapillai (in Sanskrit) 'Sampatkumara' Cheluvapillai, and so on in Karnataka inscriptions.

In this scene, Indira Parthasarathy focuses on the kind of religious spirit Ramanuja displayed in his encounter with the Turkish king. There is here an interesting definition of who a Vaishnava is—one who believes that it is only by divine connection that the world is invested with meaning. The Muslim king mocks at the polytheism of Hinduism, but Ramanuja professes a kind of monism which is not against various ways of constructing the relationship between man and God. Apart from this theological discussion, there is also a political dimension to this dialogue. The Turkish king comes across as a moderate and cultured man who is not intent upon destroying other religions and appropriating temple properties and treasures. The playwright seems to suggest that the early spirit of Islamic invasion had certainly petered out by the time of Ramanuja's visit to the Turkish sultanate.

Alkondavilli Govindacharya has extensively argued, citing semi-historical sources, that Ramanuja could not have gone all the way to Delhi to retrieve the idol of Sampat Kumara, for in those days any Turkish ruler of the north was referred to as 'Delhi Sultan'.

It is probable that Ramanuja went to the court of some Muslim chieftain or even a king who ruled north of the Hoysala region (AKVG1906 [2004: n.5 pp. 163-5]). Some historians wonder whether Ramanuja was acquainted with Islam as a religion. However, he does not seem to have shown any hostility or ill will towards the Turkish ruler. There was some unease in his interaction with the Jains. But we find that this arduous journey up north seems to have been purely motivated by devotion. He must have been far advanced in age too. The meeting with the Muslim girl who is infatuated with the image of Sampat Kumara, is somewhat filmy in dialogue, lacking in spiritual fervour as well as political pressure. The sociologically interesting detail in this otherwise sentimental scene is the appellation 'Turukka Nachiyar' given to the young Muslim girl by Ramanuja in analogy with Tamil women devotees in the Hindu Bhakti tradition. Nevertheless, Ramanuja assures the Turkish king that he will not convert his younger sister to Hinduism. In several Vaishnava temples, even today, there is a shrine for a Muslim lady. Hence, what Ramanuja prophesies in this scene is attested by later developments in Vaishnavism. The playwright himself says in his Preface that the Lord in Srirangam when he pays an annual visit to the shrine of Bibi Nachiyar (Turukka Nachiyar) wears a lungi like a Muslim youth. S.Kalyanarama Iyengar refers to the folk memory and tradition regarding the Turkish girl. She is also known as Varanandini. She was following her favourite idol of Sampat Kumara in a palanquin. However, 3 miles before reaching the foothills of Tirunaryaanapuram, she disappeared from the palanquin. When Ramanjua was asked about it, he said she became a flame and entered into the sanctum to turn into an idol at the foot of Sampat Kumara. At that spot, over a rock, there is a small shrine at which people worship 'Hokulamma' (Kalyanrama Iyengar 1978: 341). The encounter with the Turkish sultan, at any rate, confirms that Ramanuja was conciliator par excellence in all his activities.

SCENE 10

There is a sense of the carnivalesque in this scene located at Melukote after the Sampat Kumara idol has been installed and festivals initiated.

The Panchamas get the honour of carrying the Lord. There is much music and dancing. Here, popular culture and art forms are given free play by royal and religious authorities. Indira Parthasarathy compacts twelve years of Ramanuja's stay in the Karnataka region into a couple of prominent scenes. Scene 10 is a kind of epilogue to the Karnataka period. By this time, Ramanuja has succeeded in firmly establishing the new Vaishnava faith in Karnataka and he had to go back to Srirangam.

ACT IV

Historically speaking, Ramanuja returned to Srirangam after his Karnataka mission was accomplished. However, legend claims that he got a message from Srirangam that the dogmatic Chola king had died of a carbuncle in his neck. Hence he was known as *Krimikanta Cholan,* 'worm-necked Chola'. His death pleased Ramanuja no end, according to some of the sources, and M.S. Govindasamy points out that a couple of sectarian accounts even say that Ramanuja, as he was fleeing, prayed that some deadly disease should visit the king and later when he heard that the king was dead, he was elated. This, in the historian's opinion, is unbecoming of such a great and generous-minded acharya. He argues that in all his dealings, even according to traditional narratives, Ramanuja was a highly refined genial soul, and even forgave those who did him harm such as his guru Yadava Prakasa. While it is understandable that the acharya was anxious about the state of affairs in the Tamil country, one wonders whether he could have been driven to such mean-mindedness even in extremity. Another aspect that bothers a modern-day reader is Ramanuja's rather belated enquiry about what happened to Kuresa and Maha Purna who were taken away to the king's court. Of course, those were days of slow communication and difficult journeys. He might not have come to know about the cruel happenings at the Chola court for a considerable period.

Indira Parthasarathy ends the play not with the death of Ramanuja but with Ramanuja bestowing upon Kuresa's son, Parasara, the status of his successor in the mutt. In drama, we cannot have a cradle-to-grave narration. The aged Ramanuja in this scene expresses satisfaction that he has fulfilled the three wishes of Alavandar. The last one was the commentary on *Vyasasutra* which Ramanuja says he has completed with the help of Kuresa and Andalamma. There is a clue to Ramanuja's span of life, especially in the completing of the commentary. Did he finish his *Sri Bhashyam* before he fled to Karnataka or did he finish it after he returned to Srirangam?

APPENDIX 1

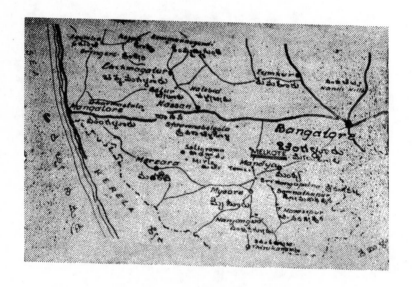

Map of Karnataka Region Visited by Ramanuja.
(*Source*: S. Kalyanarama Iyengar, *Sri Ramanujar Charitra Araaichi Mahimai*, Siddha Research Home, Sri Visishtadvaita Pracharini Sabha, 1978, p. 374.)

APPENDIX 2

1

SĀLIGRĀMA

On a beam of the doorway of the Śripādatīrtha pond opposite the Rāmānujāchārya temple.

1. Rāmānujāya namaḥ ... triyagāsan-aṃbhōruhāśrayā jagaṃmaḷa manōjayaṃ stam-anujaṃ ...

2. sti śrī śrī Sāligāveya śrīvaishṇavariṃge Srīraṅgada maṭadali Eṃbāruṃ Āḷanuṃ Āchānuṃ Śrī pratapa ...

3. . ru .... vaṇa .... hadā .... geysinaleṃdu tama Tirumāḷa amūrīṃge baralu navya prasāda vara ...

This broken and worn out inscription is in characters of c. 12th century. It seems to confer some privileges upon the Śrivaishṇavas of Sāligāve (Sāligrāma) by Embār, Āḷān and Āchchān of the maṭha at Śrīraṅga. This latter is obviously identical with the maṭha at Śrīraṅgam one of the foremost Śrivaishṇava centres of Tamilnāḍu. Embār, Āḷān and Āchchān of the record may be identified respectively with Gōvinda, Ānandāḷvān (Anantasūri of Kiraṅgūr) and Kaḍāṁbi Āchchān.

(*Source*: B.R. Gopal, *Sri Ramanuja in Karnataka*, Sundeep Prakashan, 1983.)

APPENDIX 3

23

Stone paved into the floor of the Yatirāja-maṭha

1. śrīmatē Rāmānujāya namaḥ
2. Naḷa-saṃvatsarada Mārgaśira śu 12
3. Guruvāradalu śri vayikuṃṭha
4. vardhanakshētradalu nelasuhadu
5. Nārāyaṇadēvara nirūpadi
6. ṃda Ayivatibarū Teraka
7. ṇāṃbiya Chenapa-śeṭṭiyara
8. makaḷu Aḷagiya Maḷavāḷadāsa
9. rāda Kēṭiyappa-seṭṭiyaru
10. Rāmānujakūṭake biṭṭa grā
11. ma . . . . vanabaḷi 1 Kāmarasapu
12. ra 1 aṃtu grāma 2 Harahina Kēta
13. nahaḷiyalu gada kha 5 yīshṭu
14. nū . . māḍikoṃḍu . nā
15. lku . . śrīvayishṇavaru ama
16. durśanake kaṭṭaḷeyanū Bhāshya
17. kāṟara saṃnidhiyali naḍaśi bahe
18. ü eṃdu bareśi . . lā-sā
19. dhana

This record of 13th century registers a gift of two villages, Kāmarasanapura and another whose name is lost, as also wet land of the sowing capacity of 5 *kha* (*khaṇḍugas*), in Kētanahaḷḷi by Kēṭiyappa-seṭṭi, son of Chennappa-seṭṭi of Teraka-ṇāmbi, at the instance of the fifty two *mahājanas* of the temple of Mēlukōṭe for feeding *śrīvaishṇāvas* in the Rāmānujakūṭa attached to the shrine of the Bhāshyākaṟa, i.e. Rāmānuja. The record is dated the cyclic year Naḷa, Mārgaśira śu. 12, Thursday, corresponding to 1256 A.D., November 30. This might be the intended date. The donor is described as Aḷagiya-maḷavāḷadāsa and it is possible to interpret that he was a disciple of Aḷagiyamaṇavāḷan.

(*Source*: B.R. Gopal, *Sri Ramanuja in Karnataka*, Sundeep Prakashan, 1983, pp. 62–3.)